Implementation of School-Based Management in Indonesia

Georges Vernez, Rita Karam, Jeffery H. Marshall

Sponsored by the World Bank

RAND EDUCATION

This work was sponsored by the World Bank. The research was conducted in RAND Education, a unit of the RAND Corporation.

Library of Congress Cataloging-in-Publication Data

Vernez, Georges.
  Implementation of school-based management in Indonesia / Georges Vernez, Rita Karam, Jeffery H. Marshall.
    p. cm.
  Includes bibliographical references.
  ISBN 978-0-8330-7618-2 (pbk. : alk. paper)
  1. School management and organization—Indonesia. 2. School management and organization—Indonesia—Statistics. 3. Educational planning—Indonesia. I. Karam, Rita. II. Marshall, Jeffery H. III. Title.

  LB2953.V47 2012
  371.209598—dc23

                                                            2012020643

Published 2012 by the RAND Corporation
1776 Main Street, P.O. Box 2138, Santa Monica, CA 90407-2138
1200 South Hayes Street, Arlington, VA 22202-5050
4570 Fifth Avenue, Suite 600, Pittsburgh, PA 15213-2665
RAND URL: http://www.rand.org/
To order RAND documents or to obtain additional information, contact
Distribution Services: Telephone: (310) 451-7002;
Fax: (310) 451-6915; Email: order@rand.org

Preface

As part of a broad decentralization of governance responsibilities to districts, the Indonesian government established school-based management (SBM) in 2003. SBM is a form of education governance that grants responsibilities to, and authority for, individual school academic operations to principals, teachers, and other local community-based members. The expectations are that local, and often shared, decisionmaking will lead to more efficient and effective policies and programs aligned with local priorities, which in turn will lead to improved school performance and student achievement. To further encourage more school autonomy, a grant program to schools, the school operational funding program (*Bantuan Operasional Sekolah* or BOS), was established in 2005. BOS provided a per-student amount (rupiah [Rp] 400,000 per student in 2010 for elementary schools) to all schools and comes with few strings attached, allowing it to be disbursed according to local priorities.

Because of the limited scope of past research on the implementation and effects of SBM in Indonesia, eight years after it was first implemented the World Bank commissioned the RAND Corporation to undertake a study whose principal aims were to (1) provide a nationwide quantitative and qualitative status report on the implementation of SBM, (2) identify factors associated with successful practices of SBM, and (3) assess the effects of SBM on student achievement. The study was carried out in 2010 and 2011.

This final report provides a nationwide account of the status of SBM in Indonesia. It is based on face-to-face surveys of principals, teachers, school committee (SC) members, and parents in 400 elementary schools; surveys of district staff in 54 districts; and a case study in a subsample of 40 schools.

The study was conducted by RAND Education, a unit of the RAND Corporation, and was sponsored by the World Bank. The findings of this study should be of interest to the government of Indonesia, its Ministry of National Education, education administrators, principals, teachers, and all those in Indonesia and elsewhere who are implementing or thinking about implementing some form of school-based management.

The principal author of this work (Georges Vernez) may be contacted by email at vernez@rand.org or by phone at 310-393-0411, extension 6211. For more information on RAND Education, contact the Director, Darleen Opfer, who can be reached by email at dopfer@rand.org; by phone at 310-393-0411, extension 4926; or by mail at RAND Corporation, 1776 Main Street, P.O. Box 3138, Santa Monica, CA 90407-2138. More information about RAND is available at www.rand.org.

Contents

Figures

Tables

Summary

In 2003, the Indonesian government began to decentralize the governance of its primary and secondary education system as part of its decentralization of responsibilities to district governments (regencies) initiated to strengthen the country's democratic processes. Schools were given authority to manage their operations independently according to student needs and were asked to engage the local community to improve the quality of education. This decentralized form of school management, often called school-based management, required a major shift in how people think about schooling and a significant improvement in the capacity of principals, teachers, and the community to provide leadership, develop programmatic alternatives to meet local educational needs, and engage parents and the community in the governance of schools.

Nationwide implementation of SBM in Indonesia received monetary and technical assistance from various international organizations including the World Bank; the United Nations Children's Fund; the United Nations Educational, Scientific and Cultural Organization (UNESCO); the Asian Development Bank; the U.S. Agency for International Development (USAID); the Australian Agency for International Development; the Japan International Cooperation Agency; and the Embassy of the Kingdom of the Netherlands. In spite of this high level of support and attention, little is known about the status of implementation of SBM eight years after it was first implemented. For this reason, the World Bank asked RAND to conduct the first nationwide comprehensive assessment of SBM implementation and, as needed, to develop recommendations for its improvement.

The Indonesian SBM Program

SBM programs have been implemented in many developed and developing countries and have taken many forms, although they have rarely been implemented nationwide as in Indonesia. SBM programs typically differ along the continuum of two main dimensions: the scope of responsibilities and the authority delegated to the school and who this authority is devolved to—e.g., the school, an outside board, or another independent institution.

The Indonesian version of SBM was intended to give schools broad authority to design, implement, and manage their educational programs and classroom instruction in accordance with local social norms and culture. However, the hiring and assignment of civil service teachers (*pegawai negeri sipil* [PNS]) remain the responsibility of the central government. Although authority was devolved to schools, schools were also mandated to establish an advisory school committee (SC) whose functions include giving input on school educational policy and programs, budget plans, and teacher training; increasing society's attention and commitment to quality education; motivating parents to participate in their children's education; collecting money in support of education; and supervising educational policy and program implementation. To promote transparency, SC members were to be elected and broadly representative of the community.

Schools were directed to formulate a school vision, mission, and goals on "the basis of inputs from all stakeholders including the SC and decided by a teaching board meeting chaired by the principal" and to develop a four-year and an annual plan, the latter to be approved by the teaching board and subject to the input of the SC. Monitoring of school management was to be exercised by the SC on a regular and continuous basis, and supervision over academic management was to be exercised by the principal and the district. Schools were also required to assign a member of the teaching staff to respond to complaints and to requests for information from the public. The education district's role was limited to *validating* the plans and *coordinating* and *supervising* the development of their schools' curriculum.

In 2005, a block grant, the *Bantuan Operasional Sekolah* program, was established to further support the autonomy of schools by providing them with resources that they could flexibly disburse according to school priorities. Another objective of this program was to improve access to education by freeing poor students from school fees. The block grant amount is based on student enrollment, providing a fixed amount per student, about U.S. $43 in 2010, to all elementary schools. Before this, school operational costs other than teacher salaries were covered by parental fees.

Objectives and Methods

The study had four main objectives:

- conduct a formative assessment of the implementation of SBM
- associate "intermediate" SBM outcomes (authority, participation, transparency) with features of the district, schools, teachers, and communities
- analyze the effects of SBM and other school factors on student achievement
- provide recommendations for policy interventions and future research.

To address these questions, we surveyed principals, teachers, SC members, and parents in a random sample of 54 out of 470 districts, drawn from all seven regions of Indonesia. Within selected districts, a 2 percent random sample of schools was selected. The sample was weighted to represent the universe of elementary schools for the whole of Indonesia. In each selected school, we surveyed the principal, six teachers (randomly selected, one per grade), the SC chair and one member (randomly selected), and six parents (randomly selected, one per grade). In addition, in each of the 54 districts, we surveyed the head of the district, the head of one randomly selected subdistrict, the chair of the district's education board, and the head of the district's supervisors. Respondents were surveyed face-to-face in April and May 2010. We also developed and administered Bahasa language and mathematics tests to one fifth-grade class in each surveyed school.

The surveys were complemented with an in-depth case study of a stratified randomly selected subsample of 40 schools. For logistical reasons, sampling of the case study schools was limited to the three regions of Java, Sulawesi, and Sumatera. In each school, we interviewed the principal and conducted focus groups with up to four teachers and four parents (randomly selected), SC members (the chair plus three randomly selected members), and BOS team members.

Two study limitations need to be highlighted. First, our findings are based on self-reports from the various respondents and are subject to imprecision and, most importantly, social desirability biases. The latter may have been somewhat mitigated by the confidentiality of the survey. In addition and where possible, we sought to identify such biases by asking similar questions of providers of input or services (such as training) and of recipients of these services. We expected that the first might be more positively biased than the second. Also, when there was disagreement between survey and case study responses, we gave more weight to the case study responses. In the case study, respondents could be probed to clarify their answers and, hence, were less likely to be biased by social desirability. A second limitation is that data were collected at only one point in time so that changes over time could not be described.

Findings

Current Status of SBM Implementation

We found that most principals perceived that they had autonomy over their school's operational, budgetary, programmatic, and instructional decisions consistent with the intent of the central government's decentralization of governance. Principals said that they even had autonomy in hiring and assigning teachers, even though these functions remained under the authority of the central government, at least for PNS teachers. One potential reason for this perception is that schools have been hiring non-PNS teachers with BOS funds, the latter accounting for nearly one-third of the country's teacher force. Most teachers also said that they had full autonomy in their classrooms including over their choice of instructional methods, groupings of students, and sequence in which they teach the curriculum.

Although they reported having autonomy over their school decisions, principals also reported that they did not take advantage of it by making significant programmatic or instructional changes. And when they did, they typically sought the approval of their district supervisor or other appropriate district staff. One indicator of the reluctance of schools to make independent decisions was the almost complete uniformity in schools' stated goals and priorities and actions taken to improve student performance. This finding is consistent with the reported high level of influence that many districts continued to have in all areas of school managerial and programmatic decisions, including the choice of textbooks and curriculum.

Although most principals consulted with teachers, district staff, and other school principals before making decisions, community and, more broadly, parental participation in school decisionmaking and school affairs remains to be achieved. SC members rarely met and were rarely actively involved in school decisionmaking processes, including the setting of the school's mission, the allocation of BOS funds, and the development of an annual plan. Commonly, the SC chair was simply asked to sign off, as required by governmental guidelines, on decisions already made—which they did mostly without asking any questions. Principals mainly viewed the SC as just an intermediary between the school and parents, even though SCs rarely held meetings with parents to get their input. In turn, SC members' attitude was one of noninterference in school matters and deference to the school staff. Lack of knowledge and time were other reasons given by both principals and SC staff for the lack of SC involvement in school affairs.

As for parents more generally, their attitude was also one of deference to school staff. Schools never held meetings with parents, except when the latter were invited to pick up their children's report cards.

Most principals and teachers reported that they felt little to no pressure from parents and the community at large to improve their school's performance.

At the same time, districts were said to continue to exercise a high level of influence on school policies and practices. Principals said that they rarely made a decision without seeking district approval, in part out of fear of making a mistake or of appearing authoritarian. District influence was said to equal or exceed that of teachers across various areas of school management and academic areas, with the exception of classroom instructional practices. Another indicator of district influence is the high frequency of meetings that principals reported having with district staff.

District and school activities that would promote external transparency and accountability were few. Little information, including on BOS resource allocation, was said to be formally provided or received by either SC members or parents. School sharing of information with SC members was similarly said to be nil or insufficient by nearly half of SC members. Districts, mainly through their supervisors, made frequent (more frequently than quarterly) monitoring visits to schools— however, these visits reportedly focused mainly on administrative school and classroom matters. Although heads of supervisors said that supervisors observed teachers' instruction, half of teachers received no feedback and another quarter received it only once or twice a year. When they received feedback, it was more in terms of what teachers should be doing (e.g., increase student achievement or increase their use of teaching props) and less in terms of how they should do it.

Resources and School Capacity to Implement SBM

We found that principals, teachers, and SC members had insufficient understanding of what SBM required of them and of the functions attributed to the SC, possibly contributing to the mixed implementation of SBM by schools. For instance, they understood SBM's theory and overall purposes (school autonomy, community participation) but not necessarily the responsibilities and the required actions they implied. Most principals and SC members had some misconceptions regarding the functions of the school committee. In addition, a majority of principals said that they were not well prepared to provide effective leadership and perform such SBM-related activities as formulating a vision for school staff, developing a plan for school academic improvement, and making decisions on school curriculum. Similarly, a majority of teachers reported they were not well prepared to plan effective lessons and use various instructional methods and, hence, were unprepared to try alternatives to their routine instructional practices. District staff members, including supervisors, were even less positive about principal and teacher preparation.

The availability of discretionary resources differed greatly across schools, with some schools reporting receiving less funding per student than provided by the central BOS (about U.S. $43 per student in 2010) and other schools receiving far in excess of it. The latter schools were receiving additional resources from their provincial, district, or local government. Contributions from parents and other sources were minimal. Overall, the average school received 83 percent of its discretionary funding from the BOS program.

District Support for SBM Implementation

Districts and nongovernmental agencies reported that they offered, or were said to offer, many opportunities for socialization or training on SBM, the BOS program, school planning, and instruction. However, more than half of principals reported that they either had not received any training in the past year or found it insufficient, especially with regard to such SBM-related activities as developing a school's vision and work plan, making best use of budget resources, developing the curriculum, working with the SC, or involving parents and the community in supporting the school. Similarly, about two-thirds of teachers said that they had not received any training in the past year or that the training was insufficient in such areas as using various instructional methods, teaching their subject matter, and planning lessons more effectively or preparing the school plan. When teachers received training, it amounted to only one to four days of training over the year. Socialization of SC members about their roles and responsibilities was even more sporadic, with half of districts not offering such training and a majority of SC members reporting not receiving any socialization over the past two years.

When asked what assistance they most needed to make their school better, principals and teachers most frequently mentioned improvements to their school's physical facility and support for teachers. School facility upgrades desired ranged from more chairs and tables to more classrooms and rooms for a library, laboratory, or health unit. The support desired for teachers included more training on teaching methods, academic content, and thematic approaches to teaching the curriculum. It also included greater access to such teaching aids as maps, scales, visual aids, and science and mathematics kits.

Factors Associated with SBM and Student Outcomes

We found few district and school characteristics to be associated with measures of SBM implementation, the share of discretionary funds allocated to instruction, teacher attendance, or student achievement. Higher principal education was associated with greater principal influence on school operations and a higher share of discretionary budget allocated to instruction. Similarly, higher principal preparedness was associated with greater principal influence on school operations and with higher student achievement. Principal preparedness is a self-reported measure of how well prepared the principal was to provide effective leadership, plan for school academic improvements, make decisions on school curriculum, and supervise and evaluate teachers.

The higher the number of training days teachers received and the higher the usefulness of teacher working group (KKG) meetings, the greater the teacher influence on instruction and school operations. Also, certified teachers were associated with higher student achievement.

Schools that offered opportunities for parents to file complaints and were responsive to parents' opinions and feedback and schools that provided written information on school activities were associated with a larger share of their discretionary funds being spent on instruction and a higher likelihood of receiving input from parents.

Schools receiving funds from their provincial or district governments, in addition to the funds received from the central government BOS program, were associated with a larger share of their discretionary resources being spent on instruction. However, not all schools received such additional funding, leading to wide differences across schools in the amount they had available per student.

Last, we did not find that implementation of SBM practices or the share of discretionary funds schools spent on instruction was associated with student achievement. It may be that implementation of SBM, at least so far, has not resulted in major changes in school practices, as suggested in this report.

Recommendations

Improving the implementation and outcomes of SBM in Indonesia will require expanding principal, teacher, and SC member capacity to implement SBM; increasing school staff ability to make operational and instructional changes; and developing district capacity to support schools and SBM.

Expanding SC, Principal, and Teacher Capacity to Implement SBM
Make it easier for SC members to participate in school affairs by requiring that schools meet with the SC during hours convenient for their members and provide SC members with an incentive to participate in the form of a small stipend to cover transportation and other meeting costs.

Upgrade the knowledge of SC members by providing training about the goals and purposes of SBM, about SC functions, and about how to fulfill these functions, including how to conduct meetings, develop a school vision, engage in participatory planning and budgeting, and monitor school indicators to assess school activities. The above knowledge and guidelines should be codified in a manual made available to SC members for easy reference. To be effective, training will need to be ongoing and of sufficient intensity.

Increase the authority of the SC by considering implementing one or more of the following measures:

Clarify the policy regarding SC fund-raising activities: Most SCs and schools behave as if fund-raising from parents were prohibited. If it was not the intent of the central government to entirely do away with fund-raising by SCs, this should be communicated clearly.

Link the school and the SC with the village council: Pradhan et al. (2011) have shown the potential that reaching out to education stakeholders outside the school committee—and especially the village council—has in improving student learning.

Give the SC authority over the hiring and firing of principals or teachers: Programs that have given school committees this authority have been found to increase council and parental participation in school matters, including school planning and administration of the budget.

Provide the SC, parents, and the public with comparative information on schools to help parents make informed school choice decisions. To further help parents, schools should be held accountable; competition should be encouraged among schools; and information should be provided comparing their school's overall performance and other characteristics, such as class size and academic and extracurricular programs, with those of other schools in their locality, district, and the nation.

Upgrade principal and teacher capacity to implement SBM by considering the following:

Provide principal leadership training: With the Indonesian form of SBM, the principal is the most important stakeholder. His or her actions determine the extent to which school decisions will be participatory and focused on operational and instructional improvements. The objective of principal leadership training should be to provide an understanding and full appreciation of the practices that make effective leaders.

Provide principals and teachers with professional development on the SC role and on effective SBM practices: In addition to providing professional development in these areas, both principals and teachers need to develop skills in conducting SBM-related activities, including how to conduct school and student need assessments; formulate a school's vision, mission, and objectives; engage in participatory planning; develop a curriculum; prepare a budget; and implement school improvements. To be most effective, this professional development should be provided to all teachers in the school or cluster of schools at the same time.

Clarify the authority devolved to the school: The SBM guidelines decreed by the Ministry of National Education are ambiguous, leaving room for the district to continue to play its traditional authoritative role over schools. As we found, schools are generally shy about doing anything that may not be approved by their district. The standards for SBM should be clarified to unambiguously indicate devolvement of authority to schools. The role of the district should be limited to that of enabler and monitor of SBM implementation and school performance (see "Develop District Capacity to Support SBM," below).

Broaden school autonomy: Given that the quality of teachers plays a significant role in setting the conditions for student learning, transferring the authority to hire and fire PNS teachers from the central government to school principals should be considered. This would not be new to principals who already have been hiring and overseeing non-PNS teachers used to complement PNS teachers. Principals would thus gain more flexibility to balance the school's teacher workforce with programmatic needs.

Increase School Staff Ability to Make Operational and Instructional Changes

The measures discussed above may lead to stakeholders' increased participation in school operations but not necessarily to programmatic, curriculum, or instructional changes that would be expected to affect student learning more directly. To increase the ability of schools to implement curriculum and instructional changes, we recommend considering the following three measures:

Assess the Need for Professional Development and Provide It If Required. To make their schools better, principals and teachers said that they needed more training in academic content, teaching methods, and thematic approaches to teaching the curriculum. Research also suggests that teacher knowledge of their subject matter is associated with higher student achievement. And, although Indonesian teachers are being asked to use a more student-centered form of teaching, so-called active learning or PAKEM,[1] they have received little or no training to apply it in the classroom, and research suggests that this potentially results in poorer instruction. Given limited resources and extensive training needs, we recommend that a teacher training needs assessment be conducted first to help set priorities. Research also suggests that to be most effective, all teachers in a single school or cluster of schools should be trained at the same time.

Expand Access to Teaching Aids. Other support that teachers said they needed to improve the quality of their schools includes having greater access to teaching props, from simple maps, scales, and visual aids to science and mathematics kits. These props help students understand concepts visually and may lead to gains in instructional time, allowing teachers to cover the curriculum in greater depth.

Address Resource Disparities Among Schools. Effective development and implementation of programmatic improvements depend, in part, on whether schools have sufficient resources to finance them. As this study found, schools differ markedly in the discretionary resources available to them in part because of unequal contributions made by provinces and districts, raising the question of the role that each level of government (provincial, district, and local) ought to play in financing education. A first step in addressing this question would be to collect more detailed information on the current financing of education by districts and provinces and their fiscal capacity.

Develop District Capacity to Support SBM

Providing the support necessary to upgrade school stakeholders' capacity to implement SBM and make educational improvements as suggested above will also require altering the role of the district to that of an *enabler of change*. Districts will need to expand their capacity to provide *ongoing* technical assistance and staff development to principals,

---

[1]   PAKEM stands for *Pembelajaram yang Aktif, Kreatif, Efektif dan Menyenangkan* or active, creative, effective, and joyful learning.

teachers, and SC members. As noted by our respondents, providing occasional socialization for one or two days, as is the current practice, is not sufficient for stakeholders to fully understand the changes required in their actions. The functions of district supervisors should principally be to monitor school SBM implementation and improvements and provide supportive technical assistance and mentoring. Research has shown that providing principals and teachers with ongoing access to expert advice and consultation after training is completed is more effective than training alone. To take on this role, supervisors themselves will need adequate training before they can provide this ongoing support.

Setting Priorities and Incremental Implementation of Recommendations

Developing SC and school capacity and altering the role played by districts will require both time and additional resources. Although our recommendations are based on research best practices, we recognize that they have not always been consistently found to be effective in all cultural and educational environments. Considering limited resources and the uncertain effectiveness of recommended actions, policymakers should (1) carefully set priorities for which recommendations to implement and in what sequence and (2) implement the selected measures experimentally and incrementally, involving a limited number of districts and schools at a time to learn about the implementation challenges and issues involved and to ascertain effectiveness. For instance, we recommend focusing first on increasing school staff capacity to make operational and instructional changes along with restructuring the role of districts and doing so initially experimentally in a few districts and schools in clusters within those districts. Once experience has been gained in a few districts and potential implementation issues have been addressed, implementation could be expanded to a few more districts and schools at a time.

Acknowledgments

The study team is grateful to officials and staff in the Ministry of National Education for their overall support of this study. Special thanks go to Bapak Didik Suhardi, Director for Junior Sector Education, and his staff. We are particularly grateful to Bapak Budi Susetyo, who was always there to help, and who smoothly facilitated the key activities under this study. We thank all the district and municipality government staff, school principals, teachers, school committee members, and parents who responded to our surveys and shared with us their experiences and concerns about SBM and other educational matters.

We want to thank the members of the World Bank team who managed the study, including Dandan Chen (Task Team Leader, Senior Economist, Human Development Sector Department, East Asia and Pacific Region [EASHE]), Siwage Negara (Operations Officer, EASHE), and Imam Setiawan (Research Analyst, EASHE). Important contributions were also made by Ratna Kesuma (Senior Operations Officer, EASHE), Andrew Ragatz (Consultant, EASHE), and Javier Luque (Senior Education Economist, Human Development Sector Department, Latin America and Caribbean Region). Dyah Kelaswaro Negraheni provided the most efficient team support.

This report also benefited greatly from inputs and comments by the participants at consultation workshops. Participants at a briefing of preliminary survey results held in Jakarta provided useful insights on interpreting our early findings and first planted the idea of conducting an in-depth case study to help in this regard. We are most appreciative.

Bondan Sikoski and her team of interviewers and data processors at SurveyMeter deserve special recognition for their excellent survey and case study work. They traveled to far places, paid diligent attention to details, and were persistent in making sure that nearly all targeted respondents were reached.

The expertise and effort of the Indonesia Assessment Institute in designing the testing instruments are also much appreciated.

We thank our RAND colleagues Paco Martorell, Mary Fu, and Beth Katz, who helped to design the sample of districts and schools and to process the survey data.

Several people reviewed a draft of this report and made useful comments and substantive suggestions that greatly improved the final product. They include A. Al-Samarrai, Deon Filmer, Nur Hidayat, Yulia Immajati, Harry A. Patrinos, Susan Wong, and Jan Weetjans at the World Bank; Professor David Pedder, School of Education, University of Leicester; and Catherine Augustine, RAND.

Louis Ramirez typed several drafts, including this final version, with good humor and professional efficiency. We thank him.

The production of this report was made possible through the generous support of the Dutch Education Trust Fund.

The views and interpretations expressed herein are solely those of the authors. In particular, they do not necessarily represent the opinions of the Indonesian government or our sponsors.

Abbreviations

BOS	*Bantuan Operasional Sekolah* (school operational funding program)
DBE1	Decentralized Basic Education Project
GDP	gross domestic product
KKG	*kelompok kerja guru* (teacher working group)
NGO	nongovernmental organization
OECD	Organisation for Economic Co-operation and Development
OLS	ordinary least squares
PAKEM	*Pembelajaram yang Aktif, Kreatif, Efektif dan Menyenangkan* (active, creative, effective, and joyful learning)
PISA	Programme for International Student Assessment
PNS	*pegawai negeri sipil* (civil service teacher)
Rp	rupiah
SBM	school-based management
SC	school committee
UNESCO	United Nations Educational, Scientific and Cultural Organization
USAID	U.S. Agency for International Development

CHAPTER ONE

Introduction

In 2003, the Indonesian government began to decentralize the governance of its primary and secondary education system as part of its decentralization of responsibilities to regional governments (regencies) to strengthen its democratic processes. In addition to education, other areas of decentralization of authority included public work, health, agriculture, and communications (Bandur, 2007). Before this change, Indonesia was one of the most centralized nations in the world (Bjork, 2003).

With decentralization, schools were given the autonomy to manage their operations independently according to the local needs of their students and community to improve the quality of education. This fundamental restructuring of school management and devolution of authority for school operations, often called school-based management (SBM), required a major shift in how people think about schooling and a significant improvement in the capacity of school principals, teachers, and the community to provide leadership, develop programmatic alternatives to meet local educational needs, and engage parents and the community in school governance.

To help implement SBM and associated programs, the Ministry of National Education sought the assistance of various international organizations including the United Nations Children's Fund; the United Nations Educational, Scientific and Cultural Organization (UNESCO); the Asian Development Bank; the Japan International Cooperation Agency; the U.S. Agency for International Development (USAID); the Australian Agency for International Development; the Embassy of the Kingdom of the Netherlands; and the World Bank.

In spite of the hundreds of millions of dollars spent to support implementation of SBM in Indonesia, there have been only a few sporadic and localized studies of the implementation progress made over the past eight years. It is in this context that the World Bank asked the RAND Corporation to conduct the first nationwide study of the status of implementation of SBM and to develop recommendations for its improvements.

Background

The Republic of Indonesia gained its independence from the Netherlands in 1949. It consists of more than 17,000 islands scattered over both sides of the equator, about 6,000 of which are inhabited. After nearly 45 years of authoritarian rule, the country held its first free parliamentary election in 1999, following the country's worst major economic crisis. Since then, a strengthening of democratic processes has included a regional autonomy program and the first direct presidential election in 2004.

Indonesia is divided into seven main regions: Bali, Java, Kalimantan, Maluku, Papua, Sumatera, and Sulawesi (Figure 1.1). Administratively, Indonesia consists of 33 provinces, each with its own legislature and governor. The provinces are subdivided into some 500 regencies or districts, called *kabupaten* in predominantly rural areas and *kota* in predominantly urban areas.

Population and Economy

With over 238 million people, Indonesia is the fourth most populous country in the world. More than half of its population lives on the island of Java. The population is growing at about 1.1 percent per year. It is a young country, with about 28 percent of its population 15 years old or less. The median age is about 28 years. About 92 percent of the population is literate.

The official national language, *Bahasa Indonesia,* is universally taught in schools and is spoken by most of the population. In addition, most Indonesians speak at least one of several hundred local languages and dialects, often as their first language.

Figure 1.1
Map of Indonesia

SOURCE: www.worldofmaps.net/uploads/pics/provinzen_indonesien.png.
RAND *MG1229-1.1*

The Indonesian economy is dominated by the industrial sector, which produces nearly half of the nation's gross domestic product (GDP), services (37 percent of GDP), and agriculture (7 percent of GDP). However, agriculture remains the largest sector, employing some 50 percent of the workforce, with services employing about 33 percent and industry 13 percent. Unemployment was at about 6.8 percent in 2010. After experiencing a decline of nearly 13 percent in its GDP in the economic crisis of 1997–1998, the Indonesian economy has rebounded and has grown at about 6 percent per year since 2007.

Primary and Secondary Education

Two ministries are responsible for managing the primary and secondary education systems: 84 percent of the public schools are managed by the Ministry of National Education and the remaining 16 percent by the Ministry of Religious Affairs. The latter ministry oversees Islamic schools, the *madrasahs*, which differ from regular schools only in their greater emphasis on Islamic studies.

Education is compulsory to grade 9. Until 2005, the operational costs of education were partially met by parental fees. With the establishment of a block grant program in 2005, the school operational funding program (*Bantuan Operasional Sekolah* or BOS) designed to eliminate fees for students of low-income parents, education is now free for most students attending public schools through grade 9. Secondary schools continue to be partially supported by parental fees. The central government pays the salaries of public school teachers. There are about 1.6 million primary school teachers and 1.4 million secondary school teachers in Indonesia.

Indonesia has about 170,000 elementary schools (grades 1–6) and 35,000 junior high schools (grades 7–9) serving some 40 million students. At the secondary school level, about 20,000 senior secondary schools prepare students for college and for 6,000 vocational schools, which serve about 7 million students. At the primary school level, more than 90 percent of schools are public (Firman and Tola, 2008). The share of public schools decreases at the junior high school level to 44 percent and to 33 percent at the secondary school level.

Students attend school 6 days a week for 5 ½ hours daily for about 44 weeks yearly. In the larger cities, some schools have to run two shifts of 4 ½ hours each. Nearly 50 percent of students are in urban areas.

Primary school net enrollment is nearly universal (95 percent), but it declines to 66 percent at the junior high school level and to 45 percent at the secondary school level. National assessment tests are administered at grades 6, 9, and 12 and these determine whether students graduate. Student achievement is lower than that of other countries. Indonesian 15-year-old students ranked 48th out of 62 countries in reading and 51st in mathematics in the 2009 Programme for International Student Assessment (PISA) (Organisation for Economic Co-operation and Development [OECD], 2010).

Recent Education Reforms

Beginning with the enactment of Law Number 20 in 2003 on the National Education System, Indonesia began a major decentralization of school governance through the introduction of SBM, in which schools are given the autonomy to manage their schools independently. This decentralization is part of the wholesale decentralization to districts of governance responsibilities for public works, health, agriculture, and communications, among other areas (Bandur, 2007). The 2003 education law also set content and competency national standards and learning assessments. The Ministry of National Education strategic plan for 2005–2009 set three main objectives: (1) improving equity and access, (2) enhancing quality and relevance, and (3) improving governance of the education sector. To support these objectives, the Indonesian government also launched the BOS program, injecting funds directly into schools to free low-income students from having to pay fees for their basic education (grades 1–9) and to buttress SBM by giving schools more freedom on how they may allocate their operational resources. At the same time, the government set up minimum requirements for teacher certification, minimum proficiency standards for student graduation at each level of education, and national tests for grades 6, 9, and 12, the passing of which determines eligibility for the next education level (Firman and Tola, 2008; World Bank, 2011a).

School-Based Management Around the World

SBM Programs Take Different Forms

SBM programs have been implemented in many developed and developing countries and take many forms. Today, more than 800 SBM programs have been implemented in more than two dozen countries ranging from Australia and the United States to Spain, Mexico, Cambodia, and Mozambique (World Bank, 2007).[1]

Their characteristics generally differ along a continuum of two dimensions: the set of responsibilities and authority devolved to the school, and who this authority is devolved to.

Authority may be devolved over one, several, or all components of school operations including allocating the school budget, hiring and firing principal and teachers, setting the curriculum, selecting textbooks and instructional materials, improving the facility's infrastructure, and developing and implementing targeted academic and extracurricular programs. Some SBM programs delegate authority in all of these areas whereas others may delegate authority in only a few, most frequently leaving the authority for hiring and firing of principals

---

[1] For a comprehensive review of SBM programs around the world, see Barrera-Osorio, Fasih, and Patrinos (2009).

and teachers and setting the curriculum to a district or the central government.

In turn, authority may be devolved to any one or a combination of the school's principal, teachers, parents, and the community, the latter typically through the intermediary of a parent council or committee. Some SBM programs may give authority over selected school operations to the principal, with parents (through a school committee [SC]) having an advisory role; others may devolve authority entirely to an SC, elected or appointed, to which school funds are allocated directly.

Effects of SBM

The theory of SBM suggests that providing schools and local stakeholders with more authority to allocate their budget and select staff, curriculum, instructional materials, and classroom methods of instruction may lead to a better learning environment for students and staff as well as instructional innovations and academic programs that are better suited to the needs of local student populations. In turn, the combination of these changes is expected to be reflected in increased student learning.

In spite of the large number and diversity of existing SBM programs, evaluations of their effects on student achievement are few, and the extent to which a given program type is most effective remains an open question. A recent review by Bruns, Filmer, and Patrinos (2011) reviewed 20 of the most rigorous evaluations of SBM programs done in 11 developing countries since 1995.[2] The types of SBM programs evaluated ranged from those that gave full authority over school operations to a community school commission or SC, including over the choice of principal and teachers (El Salvador—Jimenez and Sawada, 2003; Nicaragua—Parker, 2005; and Nepal—Chaudhury and Parajuli, 2010), to programs in which the school committee was limited to providing advice and oversight and in which teacher hiring remained out of the control of the school (Brazil—Paes de Barros and Mendonca, 1998; Kenya—Duflo, Dupas, and Kremer, 2009; and Mexico—Skoufias and Shapiro, 2006; Murnane, Willet, and Cardenas, 2006).

---

[2]   Such studies used either an experimental design or a carefully identified control group.

The review also included SBM programs that gave school committees advisory capacity over limited school operations, such as the facility infrastructure or the allocation of additional resources provided to the school (Mexico—Gertler, Patrinos, and Rubio-Codina, 2006; Cambodia—Benveniste and Marshall, 2004; and the Philippines—Khattri, Ling, and Jha, 2010).

The findings of these evaluations were mixed across and within types of programs. Some studies found that SBM had led to an increase in student enrollment and retention and a decrease in student repetition and dropout rates, whereas others did not. Similarly, some of the studies reviewed found a positive effect on student achievement, but others did not. Reasons for such variations across SBM programs and countries have yet to be identified. Potential reasons include differences in the size of the programs (smaller programs involving a few schools may be easier to effectively implement than large programs), variations in the level of implementation of the programs, and the presence of other interventions taking place at the same time.

The Indonesian SBM Program

The intent of the SBM program in Indonesia was to provide a high level of autonomy to schools and encourage broad participation of the local community in school affairs. Act 20/2003 states:

> The management of pre-school, primary, and secondary education units shall be based on a minimum-service standard by applying principles of school/madrasah-based management.[3]

The act further expects broad community participation in school management:

> Community participation in education consists of individuals, groups, families, professional associations, private companies,

---

[3] Act 20/2003, Article 51.

and community organizations in the implementation and control of quality of educational services.[4]

It further specifies that "the community shall have the rights to provide community-based education at formal and non-formal education in accordance with the typical religion, social norms, and culture for the benefit of the community."

And it defines the authority devolved to schools by stating that "providers shall design and implement curriculum, evaluate and manage education programs and funds in accordance with community and with reference to national education standards."[5] The central government maintains authority over the hiring, assignment to schools, and firing of civil service (*pegawai negeri sipil* or PNS) teachers.

To support community participation in SBM, Act 20/2003 mandates the establishment of school committees as autonomous bodies providing a place for societal participation in education and creating conditions for transparency and accountability.

School Committees

School committees were given an advisory role in deciding and implementing school educational policy. They also were given a supporting role in financial matters; an oversight role for the purpose of transparency and accountability; and a mediating role among school, government, and the community at large.[6]

It was expected that the school committees would, among other functions:

- give input and recommendations about educational policy and programs, school budget plans, facility development, teacher training, and other school matters
- increase society's attention and commitment to quality education
- motivate parents to participate in their child's education

---

[4] Act 20/2003, Article 54.

[5] Act 20/2003, Article 55.

[6] MoNE decree Number 044/U/2002, Appendix 3.

- collect money in support of education
- evaluate and supervise educational policies and program implementation.

SC Membership. Parents, education specialists, the business sector/ industry, education professional organizations, alumni and students, and prominent figures from the community are to be represented on the SC, which is to have no fewer than nine members. The SC chair can be of any background; however, the school principal cannot chair the school committee.[7] The chair is elected by the SC members, who receive no monetary or other compensation.

Forming the SC. To ensure that the formation of the SC membership is transparent and democratic, the government specified a process by which a preparation committee of five members, including the school principal and representatives of teachers and parents, would select potential SC candidates. Inclusion of the principal on the preparation committee gives him or her a potentially dominant role in choosing committee member candidates. Elections would then be held to choose the membership of the SC from among the list of candidates.

No other guidelines were provided about how the SC should go about fulfilling its functions.

Standards for School-Based Management

In 2005, schools were provided with general standards for SBM activities that they should engage in and assignment of responsibilities for these activities (Ministry of National Education, 2007). The standards direct schools and madrasahs to formulate a school vision, mission, and goals on "the basis of inputs from all stakeholders including the SC and decided by a teaching board meeting chaired by the principal." Schools are to develop a four-year (midterm) plan and an annual plan. The midterm plan is to describe the goals with regard to the quality of graduates and the programmatic improvements to enhance the quality of graduates. The annual plan is to be managerial, covering

---

[7] The principal is not named on the decree's SC membership list and, hence, it can be assumed that the principal may not also be a member of the SC.

student affairs, curriculum and learning activities, teachers and teaching staff and their development, facilities and infrastructure, finance and investment, school culture and environment, public participation and partnership, and other programs leading to quality enhancement and development.

The two plans and the school calendar are to be prepared with the input from various stakeholders and "approved by a teaching board meeting subject to the considerations from the SC and validated by the district education office." They are also to be easily accessible to stakeholders.

However, the development of the curriculum in alignment with central government content and competency standards is the responsibility of the principal but must be coordinated, supervised, and facilitated by the district. The development of the subject syllabus is the responsibility of teachers.

The guidelines also direct schools to engage in self-evaluation to improve the quality of education. For instance, it directs schools to develop evaluation methods to be used for problem diagnosis and to provide feedback for ongoing improvements. Also, schools are to develop a proper management information system "to support effective, efficient and accountable education administration."

Monitoring of school management is to be exercised by the SC on a regular and continuous basis, and supervision over academic management is to be exercised by the principal and the district. Schools are also required to assign a member of the teaching staff to respond to complaints and requests for information from the public.

Even though the regulations assign approval responsibilities on key decisions to a teaching board as noted above, the guidelines remain ambiguous as to the real authority delegated to it; the guidelines also state "that the school principal is responsible to set the school's vision and goals, draw the plans, deciding the budget and is only directed to involve teachers and the SC in making key decisions, but not to let the teacher board decide."

Similarly ambiguous is the role of the district, which is directed to *validate* the plans and to *coordinate* and *supervise* the development of the school curriculum. It appears that the Ministry of National Education remains cautious about the amount of authority it really means to devolve to schools, using language in its standards that can enable districts to continue to assert themselves over the schools.

School Operational Funding

A major tool supporting SBM in Indonesia is the introduction of the BOS program in 2005. This program provides block grants to cover school operational costs and is based on the number of students. For elementary schools, the per-student amount grew from rupiah (Rp) 177,500 in 2005 to Rp 235,000 in 2006 and to Rp 400,000 in 2009 and 2010.[8] The amount was slightly greater for junior high schools, amounting to Rp 575,000 per student in 2010 (Ministry of National Education, 2010).[9]

The BOS program was instituted as a way to encourage student access, *especially for students from poor and less-well-off families*, to a quality education through grade 9 (middle school). Initial operational guidelines issued in 2005, however, stated a broader objective for the BOS program: to provide "assistance to schools in order that they can *exempt students from school tuition.*"[10] This initial objective statement was interpreted by many to mean that basic education would be free to all. This erroneous impression, although corrected in subsequent guidelines, has remained in the mind of most Indonesians and has prompted most schools to eliminate fees for everyone and, consequently, has impeded the raising of funds by school committees and parents.

The BOS block grants come with few strings, thereby supporting SBM by providing schools with stable funds that can be disbursed according to school priorities. BOS funds can be used for any one of 13 different activities:

- purchase and reproduction of textbooks
- remedial and enrichment learning
- financing of daily tests

---

[8]   About U.S. $43 per student in 2010.

[9]   The BOS program does not apply to secondary schools (grades 10–12). These schools continue to be partially funded with parental fees.

[10]   Before the establishment of BOS, school operations other than PNS salaries were funded by parental fees levied by schools.

- honoraria to temporary teachers and teaching staff (non-PNS)
- professional development
- consumables (e.g., notebooks, pencils, paper, subscriptions to newspapers)
- utilities payments
- school maintenance payments (e.g., painting and repair of leaking roofs, doors, windows, and sanitation facilities)
- transportation expenses for poor students
- enrollment activities and administration
- computers
- management of BOS
- audiovisual aids, learning media, typewriters, and school furniture.[11]

BOS funds cannot be used for teacher bonuses, rehabilitation of facilities, or building new rooms or buildings.

BOS funds are to be managed by a BOS management team[12] in a transparent way with the involvement of a board of teachers and the SC. The latter's chair and treasurer must sign the BOS allocation and that allocation is to be visibly posted on the school's information board. Schools are required to submit to their district quarterly reports on their expenditures. As noted above, as part of an effort to integrate the BOS program and SBM, schools must develop a budget plan in which allocation of BOS funds is an integral part along with the annual plan.

Indonesia's SBM Programs Compared

Barrera-Osorio, Fasih, and Patrinos (2009) compared various SBM programs on a continuum where a *weak* SBM program is characterized by schools having autonomy over few responsibilities and limited parental and community participation, and a *strong* SBM program is characterized by schools having autonomy over all school operations,

---

[11] These items can be purchased using BOS funds only if BOS funds remain after having met the needs of the other 12 categories.

[12] The school BOS management team includes the school principal, a treasurer appointed by the principal, and a parent who is not a member of the SC and who is elected by the principal and the SC (Ministry of National Education, 2010).

and parents or school committees have autonomy over school decisions. On this continuum, the Indonesian form of SBM can be characterized as "moderate" (Figure 1.2). On the dimension of authority devolved to schools, Indonesian schools have de jure authority on most school operations, except two: the hiring and firing of teachers and such facility improvements as adding a library, laboratory, or classroom. On the dimension of to where the autonomy is devolved, the school principal is given the authority over school operations with school committees having a weak advisory role with no resources under their control.

Studies of SBM in Indonesia

To date, few studies have been devoted to the implementation of SBM and BOS: Most are qualitative and limited in geographical scope and content. They have focused primarily on the composition and role of school committees, the use of BOS funds, and anecdotal evidence of the effects of these two programs (SMERU Research Institute, 2006

Figure 1.2
Autonomy Granted to School and Devolved to Combinations of Stakeholders, by Selected SBM Programs

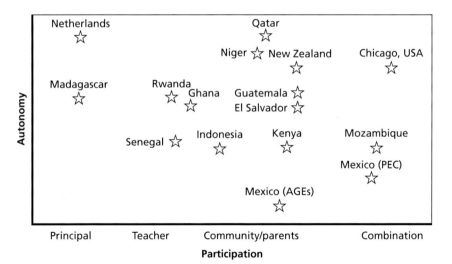

SOURCE: Barrera-Osorio, Fasih, and Patrinos (2009).
RAND MG1229-1.2

and 2008; Sweeting, Furaidah, and Koes, 2007). These studies found that school committees were of varying sizes and were mostly composed of males, with the majority of members consisting of community figures, parents, and teachers. The SC chair, possibly a respected figure in the community, often dominated committee deliberation. School management typically appointed the SC chair, so that the committee played the role of only a "rubber stamp" for the interest of the school principal.

SCs generally concentrated on the provisions of school facilities rather than on teaching and learning activities. Initially, the committees also focused on fund-raising from parents, but with the introduction of BOS, that function has diminished in importance. A number of reasons appear to have contributed to this narrow focus and weak position of the SC vis-à-vis the principal. One was the great need for renovation of many schools and the lack of SC members' relevant experience in questions of school management and learning. Another factor may have been a question of institutional legitimacy, since the principal is appointed by the district head whereas the SC is appointed locally, often with the imprimatur of the principal.

Nevertheless, anecdotal evidence suggests that the school committees had some effect in areas other than just the physical environment, such as repairing toilets, school yards, or the infrastructure. In some areas, school committees had an indirect role in ensuring that children went to school and in addressing complaints from parents, teachers, or the school. Elsewhere, teacher attendance was said to have increased and collaboration between the school and the community reportedly had improved.

More recently, Sumintono (2009) assessed SBM policies and practices in five public secondary schools in the city of Mataram, Lombok.[13] He concluded that "the limited information and support provided to schools as well as unclear regulations had resulted in those schools continuing previous practices and implementing SBM in superficial ways" (Sumintono, 2009, p. 201). The majority of principals, teachers, and SC members had received no training on SBM, the curriculum con-

---

[13] Lombok is an island at the eastern end of Java.

tinued to be centrally driven, and SC and parental involvement was limited to raising funds and providing free labor.

Two experimental programs designed to develop the capacity of schools to practice SBM were recently evaluated. The Decentralized Basic Education Project (DBE1) operated from 2006 to 2011 and provided technical assistance to schools for preparing their four-year development plans (Heyward, Cannon, and Sarjono, 2011a and 2011b; USAID, 2010). It targeted 50 districts and 24–26 schools within each district, for a total of 1,278 schools. The program trained district supervisors who, in turn, provided training and in-school mentoring. Each school received 23 days of training and 23 days of mentoring visits over a three-year period.[14] Training focused on improving leadership skills, encouraging more open and participatory approaches to school leadership, and the role of the SC in the planning process. The project helped schools prepare and implement their four-year development plans focusing on quality improvements.

A before-and-after self-evaluation of DBE1 suggests that schools that received the intervention made significant progress implementing SBM.[15] For instance, the share of schools with "good quality" plans increased from 2 to 79 percent. The plans mainly focused on teacher professional development, facility improvements, and provision of such instructional resources as computers, textbooks, and teaching aids. Transparency also increased as the proportion of schools distributing their financial reports to three or more audiences increased from 16 to 61 percent. The participation of the SC in planning and budgeting also increased. SCs were said to have participated in school planning in 13 percent of schools before the intervention—this increased to 84 percent after the intervention. Community participation was also credited with raising cash and noncash support for the schools from local communities and from village budgets. Staff attributed the success of

[14] The cost of the intervention was about U.S. $900 per school over these years. Use of supervisors who were district government employees as trainers and mentors seemed to considerably lower the cost of the intervention.

[15] This self-evaluation was completed by more than 100 persons some of whom were employed by the projects and others by local government and may have had an incentive to overestimate the successes.

the project to several factors, including involvement of all members of the school community, ongoing training and mentoring provided on-site, reliance on technical support instead of providing only funding, and built-in commitment at the provincial and district levels (USAID, 2010; Heyward, Cannon, and Sarjono, 2011a and 2011b).

The second program used a randomized experimental design to test the effect on student learning of four interventions designed to strengthen SC participation in school affairs: (1) a grant of U.S. $870 given directly to the SC with a requirement that schools develop an expenditure plan with the assistance of a facilitator who visited the school 13 times over two years; (2) two days of training for four SC members covering planning, budgeting, and steps the SC could take to support education quality; (3) structured election of SC members to achieve broad community representation; and (4) linking the SC with the village council to encourage their collaboration in making such school improvements as improving school facilities, establishing village study hours, and hiring contract teachers (Pradhan et al., 2011).[16] All schools in the experiment received the grant, regardless of which of the other three interventions they received.

Two years after implementation, the combined interventions of (1) the grant and linkage with the village council and (2) the grant, structured election, and linkage with the village council were found to have a positive effect on test scores for the Indonesian language but not for mathematics. However, the combined intervention of the grant and structured election without the linkage with the village council had no effect on learning, although it showed gains in teaching effort and the time parents spent helping children with homework.

No effects on learning were found from the combined grant and training interventions or even when these two interventions were combined with either the election or linkage with village council interventions. The authors concluded that strengthening school committees alone shows little promise but that broader SC community membership and collaboration with the village council does (Pradhan et al., 2011).

---

[16] Net of the grant of U.S. $870: The first intervention costs were estimated at U.S. $321, the second at U.S. $360, the third at U.S. $174, and the last at U.S. $125.

Research on the effects of the BOS program suggests that it diminished the SC's role as fund-raisers for their schools. At the same time, it increased school revenues, thereby increasing student access to schools, especially by the poor, as local fees were decreased or terminated. In 2009, only 8 percent of primary schools and 17 percent of junior high schools still charged fees for some parents. Primary schools used BOS funds mainly for examination activities (19 percent), extracurricular activities (14 percent), supplies (13 percent), temporary teacher honoraria (13 percent), textbooks (12 percent), and school maintenance (8 percent) (World Bank, 2011b).

At the same time, the BOS program has resulted in added administrative costs, with some schools reporting difficulties, at least initially, in preparing financial reports and in accommodating the increased monitoring and evaluation activities undertaken by a large number of institutions. Also, less than a quarter of schools placed their allocation of BOS funds on their notice boards and only one in five had established a complaint unit (World Bank, 2011b). In addition, there was some concern that providing equal subsidies to schools with predominantly wealthy parents reduced the value of the program to poor families in other schools. Another concern, and a side effect of the BOS program, was the weakening of the position of the SC as it lost its historical role as a fund-raiser (Sweeting, Furaidah, and Koes, 2007).

Study Objectives

Given the limited scope of the research on SBM in Indonesia, the World Bank commissioned RAND to undertake a study whose principal aim was to provide a *nationwide* quantitative and qualitative status report on the implementation of SBM. The study had four main objectives:

- conduct a formative assessment of the implementation of SBM
- associate "intermediate" SBM outcomes (autonomy, participation, and transparency) with features of districts, schools, teachers, and communities

- analyze the effects of SBM and other school factors on student achievement
- provide recommendations for policy interventions and future research.

Organization of the Report

Chapter Two provides an overview of the study design including our conceptual framework, sampling design, and content of data collection instruments. In Chapter Three, we describe current SBM practices for the nation as a whole with regard to school-level managerial structure, autonomy, stakeholders' participation in decisionmaking and parental voice, and accountability and transparency. The capacity of schools, principals, teachers, and other stakeholders to implement SBM is discussed in Chapter Four. Chapter Five turns to the activities that districts put in place to support SBM. In Chapter Six, we discuss selected intermediate outcomes from SBM practices, including the allocation of resources at the school level, the reported effects of BOS, the level of money and in-kind parental donations, student and teacher attendance, and parent satisfaction with their child's school. We also describe the results of our tests of student achievement. The factors associated with selected intermediate SBM outcomes and with student achievement are examined in Chapter Seven. Chapter Eight offers our conclusions and recommendations.

CHAPTER TWO

Study Design

To provide a nationwide overview of the implementation of SBM practices in Indonesia, we surveyed principals, teachers, SC members, and parents in a nationwide random sample of 54 school districts and 400 public elementary schools. In the 54 education districts (*Dinas Pendidikan*), we surveyed the head of the district office, the head of supervisors, the chair of the district's education board, and the head of one subdistrict to provide information on the role districts played in the implementation of SBM. The surveys were complemented with case studies of a subset of 40 schools in which we conducted face-to-face interviews with principals and focus groups of teachers, SC members, BOS team members, and parents.

Conceptual Framework

Implementing SBM requires that schools and stakeholders make changes in their behavior and practices, including engaging in activities for which they have no prior experience, such as planning and developing curriculum or academic programs. Inducing such changes is complex and difficult, particularly in schools where principals, teachers, parents, and the community respond to and are driven by different incentives (Berends, Bodilly, and Kirby, 2002).

Although little systematic research has been devoted to the process of change in schools implementing SBM, much research has been devoted to understanding the factors that determine the success or failure of change, particularly of comprehensive reform, in schools.[1] This literature suggests that successful implementation depends on a multitude of factors including the form, complexity, and specificity of the type of SBM chosen; the type and level of assistance provided to the school; stakeholders' understanding of the changes they are asked to implement and their capacity to make these changes; principal leadership and buy-in; and time allocated to develop and implement the changes (Bifulco, 2002; Glennan et al., 2004; Datnow, 2005). It is thus not surprising that the level of implementation of the change may differ across schools (Vernez et al., 2006) and, in turn, may affect the outcomes of the change. If there is no implementation or only partial implementation of the change, the expected outcomes are unlikely to occur (Datnow, Borman, and Springfield, 2000; McLaughlin and Phillips, 1991).

Drawing on this literature, Figure 2.1 provides a framework to describe and evaluate the status of implementation of SBM in Indonesia. At the core of the framework (the shaded box) is the status of SBM implementation in Indonesian schools, that is, the extent to which SBM as actually practiced in Indonesian schools conforms to the intended form of SBM adopted by the central government and described in Chapter One. The major implementation components include the managerial structure (i.e., the required committees and teams) implemented by schools, the level and extent of autonomy exercised by schools, the extent of stakeholder participation in school decisions, and the extent to which these decisions are communicated to stakeholders and oversight is exercised (transparency and accountability).

As shown in the shaded box in Figure 2.1, SBM implementation is moderated by the school stakeholders' capacity to implement SBM, including both time and money resources; the level of understanding they have of the changes required of them; and how well prepared they are to make those changes. School capacity, in turn, is affected by out-

---

[1]   Several studies have reviewed the implementation research of education programs and policies and need not be repeated here. For instance, see Glennan et al. (2004); Berends, Bodilly, and Kirby (2002); and Stringfield, Millsap, and Herman (1997). For an earlier review of the SBM implementation literature, see Rodriguez and Slate (1995).

Figure 2.1
Framework for Analysis of SBM Practices

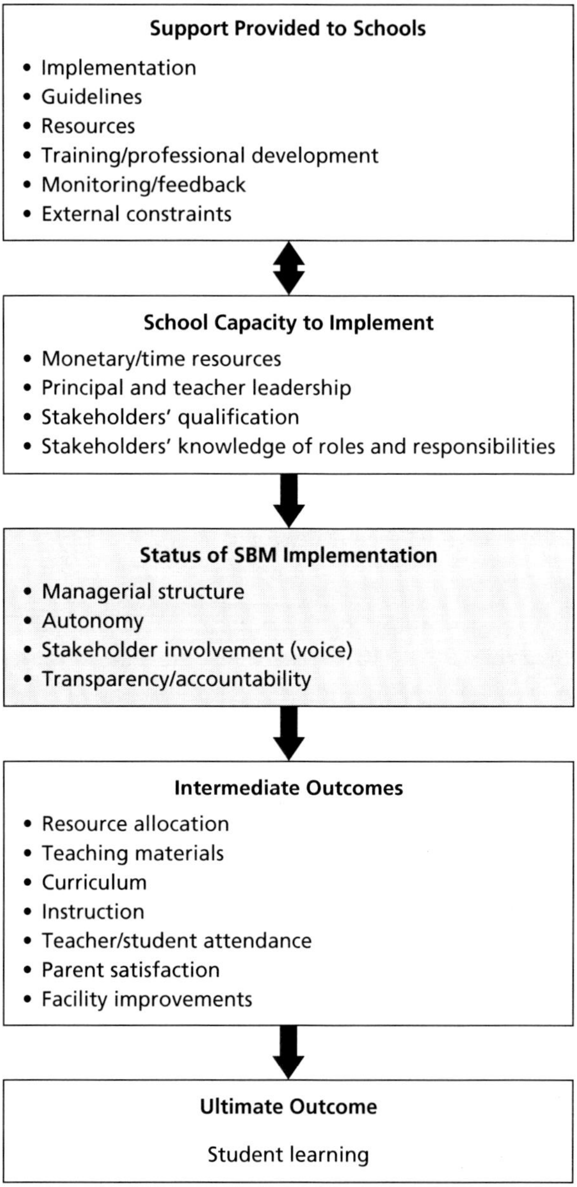

Support Provided to Schools

- Implementation
- Guidelines
- Resources
- Training/professional development
- Monitoring/feedback
- External constraints

School Capacity to Implement

- Monetary/time resources
- Principal and teacher leadership
- Stakeholders' qualification
- Stakeholders' knowledge of roles and responsibilities

Status of SBM Implementation

- Managerial structure
- Autonomy
- Stakeholder involvement (voice)
- Transparency/accountability

Intermediate Outcomes

- Resource allocation
- Teaching materials
- Curriculum
- Instruction
- Teacher/student attendance
- Parent satisfaction
- Facility improvements

Ultimate Outcome

Student learning

RAND *MG1229-2.1*

side support (e.g., districts, nongovernmental organizations [NGOs], and foundations) that may be provided to school stakeholders, such as guidelines, additional resources,[2] training, and technical assistance.

The bottom of the figure shows the types of intermediate outcomes the implementation of SBM may be expected to generate, including such changes as in the allocation of school resources, in instructional practices, and in improved teacher and student attendance. These, in turn, are expected to increase student learning.

Further elaboration and justification of the conceptual framework is provided below.

Status of the Implementation of SBM

As implementation of SBM proceeded over the past eight years, individual schools were likely to have made different decisions about which components of SBM to implement and who to consult with in making decisions, incorporating those they liked and disregarding those that they disliked (Cuban, 1998). The combination of these decisions influenced the overall consistency, level, and quality of SBM implementation in Indonesia.

We measured the status of implementation by a set of indicators of conformance to the SBM requirements, standards, and regulations set by the central government along four dimensions:

Managerial structure indicators of implementation include whether schools have established the required committees or teams (e.g., SC or teaching board) with the required composition of membership, whether SC members were elected, and the frequency of meetings held.

Autonomy indicators include whether principals and teachers perceive that they have full authority to make decisions in key school operational and academic matters.

Stakeholder involvement indicators include measures of the extent of participation of principals, teachers, SC members, parents,

---

[2] In addition to the central BOS funds, province and district governments may provide additional monetary resources to schools in the form of so-called provincial and district BOS or aid.

the community, and districts in school decisions; the respective influence of these stakeholders over school matters; the extent to which parents took advantage of parental choice; and parental pressure to improve the quality of education.

Accountability and transparency indicators include measures of district monitoring of BOS and other school activities, the frequency of monitoring by various stakeholders, feedback received and actions taken, and the type of information provided by schools to stakeholders.

School Capacity

Implementation of SBM—the way schools organized themselves as well as the decisions they made—is likely to have been affected by the amount of discretionary resources available to schools (Walker, 2002; Glennan, 1998). Principals' understanding and knowledge of the concept of SBM, their qualifications, and their leadership capacity and style are also likely to have affected the way SBM was practiced and the extent to which it was participatory (Fullan, 2001; Lindle, 1996; Osalov, 1994). Principals are not only the schools' managers—they are typically the ultimate decisionmakers and the ones who set the tone for participation and transparency in the decisionmaking process (Leithwood and Menzies, 1998). In turn, teachers' and SC members' knowledge of what SBM is and how it works, their qualifications, and their relationships with principals may have affected their involvement in SBM practices (David, 1989; Oswald, 1995). Faculty expertise and experience, or lack thereof, in engaging in such SBM-related activities as vision formulation and planning may also have affected the schools' ability to make changes designed to improve education quality (Grauwe, 2004; Peterson, 1991; Berends, 2000; Datnow and Castellano, 2000).

Support Provided to Schools

How districts supported schools in their implementation of SBM (e.g., provided information, guidelines, and formal training on what SBM is and how it works; advised school staff; and monitored school activities) is likely to have affected how SBM is practiced at the school level (Fullan 2001; Caldwell and Wood, 1988; Levine, 1991). Clear and detailed guidelines regarding roles, procedures, and expectations for all stakeholders are particularly important (Stine, 1992; Allen and Glickman, 1992), as is the strengthening of individual and school capacity to engage in such SBM-related activities as needs assessment, planning, and initiation of changes in curriculum and instruction (Ravitch and Viteritti, 1997). The amount of discretionary provincial, district, and other monetary and in-kind aid provided to schools in addition to the central BOS may also have been influential in their SBM implementation.

Intermediate and Ultimate Outcomes

With SBM, it is expected that the decisions made by schools will be more efficient and better aligned with students' needs than those that otherwise would be made under other forms of school governance (Wohlstetter and Odden, 1992; Caldwell, 2005). These decisions should be reflected initially in the priorities set by schools, the allocation of discretionary resources to support these priorities, the materials and other instructional devices made available to teachers and their students, curriculum choices, and instructional methods used in classrooms. Ultimately, the whole of these decisions and practices is expected to improve student learning (Barrera-Osorio, Fasih, and Patrinos, 2009; Leithwood and Menzies, 1998).

Survey Design

Selection of Sample Districts and Schools

The target was to select 400 elementary public schools nationwide in 54 districts. The sampling framework consisted of all districts and schools in the 2008 census of schools administered by the Indonesia Ministry of National Education in all seven regions of Indonesia, including Bali, Java, Kalimantan, Maluku, Papua, Sulawesi, and Sumatera, with the exception of schools in Aceh Province. The latter province was excluded because of the uncertainties caused by reconstruction under way after the tsunami of 2009.

Within this sampling framework, selection of districts proceeded as follows. First, within each region, the number of districts[3] to select

---

[3] We use the term "districts" to refer to both regencies (*kabupatens*) and cities (*kotas*), since they are at the same administrative levels.

was based on the region's share of Indonesia's total number of elementary schools, adjusted to ensure that in more sparsely populated regions, such as Papua and Maluku, at least three districts were selected. The number of schools in each region was chosen as the criterion for district allocation because the primary unit of observation for the study is the school (Table 2.1). Second, and before random selection of the sample districts, the number of districts to be selected within each region was divided between regencies (*kabupatens*) and cities (*kotas*) also proportionately to the number of schools in each of these two types of districts, subject to the constraint that at least one district of each type be selected in each region. This is equivalent to stratifying the sample within each district between rural and urban areas, with kabupatens considered more rural and kotas more urban. The distribution of kabupatens and kotas across the seven regions can be seen in the last two rows of Table 2.1. Selected districts are listed in Appendix A.

The appropriate number of districts of each type was then randomly selected using the Indonesia Ministry of National Education 2008 census of schools data file provided to us by the World Bank.[4]

After districts were selected, we drew a 2 percent random sample of elementary schools in each of the 54 selected districts. We also adjusted the sample of schools for accessibility reasons in one district; many schools in kabupaten Yahukimo in Papua are notoriously difficult to reach, accessible only by a 12-hour journey on foot. Hence, the sample of schools in this district was selected solely on account of accessibility.

Sampling of Teachers, Parents, and School Committee Members

Within each sampled elementary school, we aimed to interview the principal, six teachers (randomly selected, one in each grade), the chair

---

[4] In Papua, we excluded four regencies from the random selection process because they each had fewer than eight schools: Paniai, Mimika, Waropen, and Fak-Fak. In Sulawesi, we excluded regency Poso because it was considered a conflict area at the time of the survey work. Similarly, 18 regencies in Sumatera that were affected by the 2010 tsunami were also excluded from the sampling frame: Aceh Besar, Pidie, Aceh Utara, Aceh Timur, Aceh Barat, Aceh Selatan, Aceh Tenggara, Simeulue, Bireuen, Aceh Singkil, Aceh Tamiang, Gayo Luas, Aceh Nagan Raya, Aceh Barat Daya, and Aceh Jaya.

Table 2.1
District Sampling Framework

	Java	Kalimantan	Bali	Papua	Maluku	Sulawesi	Sumatera	Total
No. of elementary schools	63,349	10,435	7,467	933	1,776	13,608	28,571	126,139
Share of country's elementary schools	0.50	0.08	0.06	0.01	0.01	0.11	0.23	1.00
Share of districts	27.12	4.47	3.20	0.40	0.76	5.83	12.23	54.00
Adjusted share of districts	23	4	3	3	3	6	12	54
No. of elementary schools in kabupatens	56,719	8,656	7,014	841	1,359	12,548	24,837	111,974
No. of elementary schools in kotas	6,630	1,779	453	92	417	1,060	3,734	14,165
Share of elementary schools in kabupatens	0.90	0.83	0.94	0.90	0.77	0.92	0.87	0.89
Share of elementary schools in kotas	0.10	0.17	0.06	0.10	0.23	0.08	0.13	0.11
No. of kabupatens	20.59	3.32	2.82	2.70	2.30	5.53	10.43	48.06
No. of kotas	2.41	0.68	0.18	0.30	0.70	0.47	1.57	5.94
Adjusted no. of kabupatens	20	3	2	2	2	5	10	44
Adjusted no. of kotas	3	1	1	1	1	1	2	10

of the SC and one member (randomly selected from the list of SC members), and six parents (randomly selected, one in each grade 1 to 6).

Sample Weights

Because we oversampled some types of districts and undersampled others, we constructed sampling weights that are inversely proportional to the probability of being sampled according to the sampling scheme outlined above. The probability that a school was selected is expressed by the following set of conditional probabilities:

P(school selected: district type, region)
= P(school selected: kota/kabupaten selected)
* P(kota/kabupaten selected; region selected* P (region selected))

So the probability that a school was selected in district type and region was:

{no. of schools selected in district/2 percent of schools in district}
* {no. of district type selected/no. of district type in the region}

Applying these weights to the sample, we recaptured the representativeness of elementary schools for the whole of Indonesia by downweighting schools in oversampled districts and up-weighting schools in districts that were undersampled. This is best understood by example. In Sumatera, 10 kabupaten districts were sampled although 11 districts should have been sampled to be proportional to the share of elementary schools in Sumatera. Similarly, in one kabupaten with 399 schools, we sampled seven schools, whereas a 2 percent sample should have yielded eight schools. The above weighting scheme corrects this double undersampling by up-weighting the importance of the appropriate schools.

Data Collection

To collect data for the indicators of status of SBM implementation, school capacity, support provided to schools, and selected outcomes, survey instruments were developed for school principals, teachers, SC chairs and members, and parents, as well as for the collection of school financial and other characteristics. In addition, we developed question-naires for the head of the district, the head of the subdistrict, the head of the district's education board, and the head of the district's supervi-sors in each of the 54 sampled districts. In developing the question-naires, we were guided by the conceptual framework and, to the extent feasible, we used questions that had been validated in previous studies of SBM and in the Indonesia Family Life Surveys.

The response rate for four of the nine stakeholder surveys was 100 percent. In five of the nine surveys, however, the respondent quota could not be filled because of a shortage of available interview subjects (see Table 2.2). In the cases of subdistrict heads, SC chairs, and SC members, the reasons for non-interviews were: The entity of interest simply did not exist, or no one was available to be interviewed on the days of the survey. In the case of teachers, several schools had fewer than six teachers. Even in these instances, more than 98 percent of the targeted interviews were achieved.

The questionnaires were designed to provide indicators of school management practices; characteristics of managerial structures, such

Table 2.2
Survey Targets and Surveys Completed, by Type of Respondent

Type of Respondent	Targeted	Completed
Elementary School		
Principal	400	400
Teacher	2,400	2,352
SC chair	400	393
SC member	400	388
Parent	2,400	2,400
District		
Head of district	54	54
Head of subdistrict	54	48
Head of supervisors	54	54
Education board chair	54	54

as the existence, composition, and selection of management, BOS, budget, and school committees; stakeholder participation in school decisions; school autonomy in making final decisions in key personnel, facility, and academic areas; monitoring of activities by district and selected stakeholders; information provided to stakeholders on school activities and student performance; socialization and training provided and received by stakeholders; competency and preparation of stakeholders; and parental school choice and involvement in their child's school. Interview instruments for district and subdistrict personnel covered many of the same questions directed at school-level respondents, but they also focused on the roles and supporting infrastructure that districts and subdistricts had in place to support SBM. All survey questions were close-ended. Table 2.3 summarizes the key survey data collected by type of respondent.

In addition, using administrative sources and reporting forms required by districts, we collected data on school characteristics including student enrollment, number of PNS and non-PNS teachers, number and type of scholarships granted, hours of instruction by academic subject, and the curriculum used. We also collected information on both the 2009–2010 school operational and capital budget by source and operational and capital expenditures by category.

Finally, we developed and administered a Bahasa language and a mathematics achievement test to students in one fifth-grade class in each school. If there were two or more classes at that grade, the class to be administered the test was selected randomly by the interview team leader. In total, 8,092 students were tested in Bahasa and mathematics.[5]

Piloting and Pretesting of Survey Questionnaires.[6] The questionnaires were translated into Bahasa and piloted in December 2009 over a four-day period in one elementary school and in one district for cognitive evaluation and for validation of questions. Issues were identified

---

[5] Development of the tests was subcontracted to the Institut Asesmen Indonesia, which used developers of questions for the Indonesian national test. Specifications for the tests are included in Appendix B.

[6] SurveyMeter, an Indonesian survey company, piloted the questionnaires, trained the survey staff, fielded the study's surveys, and conducted the case study focus groups and interviews of principals.

Table 2.3
Survey Data Collected, by Type of Respondent

Type of Data	Principal	Teacher	SC Chair	SC Member	Parent	District Head	Subdistrict Head	District Supervisor Head	Education Board Chair
Respondent socio-demographics	✓	✓	✓	✓	✓	✓	✓	✓	✓
Responsibilities/services provided by district	✓					✓	✓	✓	✓
Who decides school opening/closure						✓			
Committee/team responsibilities/roles	✓	✓	✓	✓		✓			✓
Committee/team composition	✓		✓	✓		✓			✓
Selection of committee/team members			✓	✓					✓
Frequency/purpose of committee/team meetings	✓	✓	✓	✓	✓				✓
Stakeholders' influence on school affairs	✓	✓	✓	✓	✓	✓	✓		
School autonomy in school affairs	✓	✓	✓	✓		✓			
Governance style of principal	✓	✓	✓						
Knowledge of purpose of BOS	✓	✓	✓	✓	✓	✓	✓		✓
Effect of BOS	✓	✓	✓	✓		✓	✓		
Knowledge of role of SC	✓		✓	✓					
Hindrance to SBM	✓	✓				✓	✓	✓	

Table 2.3—Continued

Type of Data	Principal	Teacher	SC Chair	SC Member	Parent	District Head	Subdistrict Head	District Supervisor Head	Education Board Chair
Hindrance to SC	✓		✓						
Type/frequency of monitoring activities provided/received	✓	✓	✓	✓		✓	✓	✓	
Type/adequacy of information provided/received	✓	✓	✓	✓	✓		✓	✓	✓
Type/adequacy of training provided/received	✓	✓	✓	✓			✓	✓	✓
Preparation/competency of stakeholders	✓	✓	✓	✓		✓	✓	✓	✓
Evaluation of principal						✓	✓		
Evaluation of teacher	✓	✓							
Parental choice					✓				
Parental involvement	✓				✓				
Pressure to improve student performance	✓		✓			✓	✓	✓	
Satisfaction with school					✓				
Hindrance to increasing student performance	✓	✓	✓	✓		✓	✓		✓
Donations (money/in-kind)	✓		✓		✓				
Teacher attendance		✓							
Student attendance		✓							

with the order of the questions, with the meaning of some terms, and with the length of the questionnaires. We also learned that it would be best to interview the coordinator of supervisors instead of the district's head of supervisors because the former is generally better informed on the functions of school supervisors.

After the questionnaires were revised and shortened, they were pretested over a one-week period in January 2010. The pretest involved a full application of survey procedures in several schools and one district to identify logistical as well as survey-instrument issues. Extensive revisions were made in the Bahasa version of the questionnaires as a result of the pretest, mostly dealing with clarification of terms and length of questions. The questionnaires were then translated back into English to make certain that no important changes in the intent of the questions had been inadvertently made.

Training of Interviewers. Training of interviewers was conducted in two phases in March 2010. First, 46 team-experienced supervisors and editors[7] were trained over a four-day period on the general understanding of SBM, the purpose of each question, and the concept and terms used in the survey instruments. Second, these and 80 additional interviewers were then trained over a nine-day period. The interviewers were selected from a pool of 400 applicants who were administered a written test and interviewed. All selected interviewers held a bachelor's degree. Training consisted of a mix of classroom teaching about the purpose and content of the questionnaires and demonstration and role playing of actual interviewing. Also, an actual field practice was held at the end of the training session.

Field Data Collection. Because of the large geographical spread of the sample schools, 27 teams of five to six members were used to conduct the actual face-to-face interviews with principals, teachers, SC members, district staff, and parents; collect the administrative data; and administer the student achievement tests. Data were collected from March 27 to May 8, 2010. Each team spent three to four days at each school. Each interview was conducted by a team of two—one reading

---

[7] These supervisors and editors had, for the most part, held similar positions in previous large surveys in Indonesia.

the questions from the appropriate questionnaire and one recording the answers.

Data Entry and Cleaning

To detect data entry errors, two different clerks entered each response. The entries were then compared, an error log was created, and discrepancies were corrected by reference to the appropriate filled-out questionnaires and, in the few instances of ambiguity, by referring back to the interviewer.

Each school in the sample was asked to provide four types of financial data for the 2009–2010 school year: (1) total operational budget and main sources of revenue (hereafter, operational budget), (2) allocation of total operational budget (hereafter, operational expenditures), (3) infrastructure and facilities budget and main sources of revenue, and (4) allocation of infrastructure and facilities budget (hereafter, infrastructure expenditures). During data collection and to the extent feasible, interviewers were asked to use administrative data and reporting forms to verify the accuracy of the financial data provided by the school.

In spite of the care taken in collecting the schools' financial data, three major issues were encountered. First, the sum of individual items did not always match the reported total for 48 percent of the 454 schools for the operational and capital budgets and the operational expenditures.[8] However, the size of the discrepancies was generally small, averaging between 0.5 percent and 1.8 percent, depending on the financial category.

The second issue was that the total operational budget and total operational expenditures did not match in 27 percent of schools. These schools split evenly between schools whose operational expenditures exceeded their budget and schools whose expenditures were lower than their budget. To reconcile these discrepancies, we selected the sum of items, rather than the reported total budget or expenditures, as the "true" total. In addition, for schools whose budget exceeded expendi-

---

[8] The interviewee was not requested to report a total for the fourth budget category, infrastructure expenditures, so the sum of items was used in subsequent analyses.

tures, a surplus variable was created to capture the extra, supposedly unused, budget. Similarly, for schools whose expenditures exceeded their budget, an "unknown revenue source" variable was created to capture the extra funds.

A third issue concerned the interpretation by interviewees of the operational budget item labeled "routine expenditure for staff" and the corresponding operational expenditure item "salary for temporary staff and teachers." The former was meant to capture all funds issued by the central government for the purposes of paying salaries of PNS school staff, or civil servants. However, approximately 35 percent of the schools reported no budgeted "routine expenditure for staff." This inordinate proportion of schools suggests that some schools kept this item "off the books" whereas others included it.[9] As a result, we netted out this budget item from each school's budget and labeled it as "discretionary budget."

The expenditure item "salary for temporary staff and teachers" was meant to capture all funds expended by the school for staff and teachers, both PNS and non-PNS. Hence, and for consistency with the budget side, we also netted out the budgeted "routine expenditure for staff" from this expenditure item. The balance remaining in this item we labeled "expenditures for non-PNS staff."

Case Study Design

Selection of Schools

From the original sample of 400 schools, we selected a stratified sample of 40 schools in which to conduct in-depth interviews. We first classified schools in 12 strata along the following three dimensions: (1) low, midrange, and high levels of SBM implementation,[10] (2) low and high

---

[9] We attempted to impute salaries for PNS staff by computing the budgeted amount per teacher across schools; however, we found that the variation across schools was too large to lend credibility to this approach.

[10] The index of level of implementation was computed as a combination of three factors associated with SBM: the extent to which (1) the school had put in place a consultation managerial structure as intended by central government directives, (2) the district, province, or

expenditures per student, and (3) urban (kota) versus rural (kabupaten). For logistical and access reasons, we limited the selection of schools to three of the seven regions: Java, Sulawesi, and Sumatera. Within each of the 12 strata, we randomly selected three or four schools.

Data Collection

Separate interview protocols were developed for principals and for focus groups of teachers, SC members, BOS team members, and parents. For the teacher and parent focus groups, we aimed at randomly selecting four participants. For the SC and BOS team focus groups, we included the chair and up to three members randomly selected from the list of SC members. Participants were interviewed face-to-face by two staff members, one of whom took notes of responses to questions. The interviews were also recorded.

The protocols were designed to obtain an in-depth understanding of each stakeholder's knowledge of SBM principles and requirements, school governance, school autonomy, participation in decisionmaking, district support and accountability, and effects of SBM.

The protocols were piloted in February 2011. The pilot allowed us to correct English-to-Bahasa translation issues and the wording of questions. Actual interviews were conducted in Bahasa in April through May 2011.

Interviewers were trained in late March 2011 for a full week. They were briefed on the purpose of the study, early findings from the surveys that had been fielded in 2010, and the purpose and content of the protocols. They were also trained in the techniques of focus group interviewing and in following up on responses. Each staff member participated in at least two mock focus groups, once as interviewer and once as note-taker. After each mock focus group, interviewers were debriefed and critiqued.

---

federal office of education was involved in decisionmaking, and (3) school stakeholders were involved in making decisions in their school. For each of these three dimensions, a z-score was created and then averaged to determine the value of the index for each school.

Data Entry and Analysis

Note-takers wrote down the responses from principals and focus group participants. These notes were then reviewed and revised after listening to the recording of responses. The final notes were then translated from Bahasa to English.

The responses to each question common to more than one stakeholder were then read by an analyst and summarized in a comparative format. These detailed summaries were then used to write up a case study report for each of the main topics covered by the interview protocols: understanding of SBM, school governance, school autonomy, stakeholder participation in school decisionmaking, district support and accountability, and the effects of SBM. Responses from parent focus groups were reviewed and summarized independently and covered school governance, parental voice, and factors that would make their children's schools better.

Study Limitations

In interpreting the findings of this study, two limitations should be kept in mind. First, although we sought to ask mainly questions of fact, the findings are based on self-reports from our various respondents and are subject to imprecision and to social desirability biases. Imprecision occurs if, for instance, an individual estimates rather than accurately recalls certain quantities, such as the number of professional development hours completed. Still, insofar as a respondent's reporting precision is unrelated to other relevant characteristics about the individual or his or her school, imprecision should not bias the results. In contrast, social desirability bias may result if respondents systematically provide answers that they believe will present them or their school in a positive light rather than providing the most accurate factual answer or opinion. This tendency may have been mitigated to some extent by the confidential nature of the survey, but, to the extent that it occurred, it may have resulted in some biased (e.g., deceptively positive) findings. Where possible, we sought to identify such biases by asking similar questions from providers of input or services (such as training) and from recipients of these services. We may expect that the first may be more positively biased than the second.

Also, we covered the same topics in the case studies as in the surveys and could compare responses from the same type of respondents, namely, principals, teachers, and SC chairs. We identified several instances of survey responses that differed from case study responses, which we note in the appropriate chapters of this report. Even though the findings from the case studies cannot be generalized at the national level as the survey findings can, they suggest that survey respondents were generally more positive about the implementation of SBM and other practices than were case study respondents.

A second limitation is that the surveys were conducted at a single point in time—the spring of 2010. The analysis therefore offers a snapshot of SBM practices as a cumulative outcome of nearly eight years of experience since it was first introduced in a few districts and schools and, shortly thereafter, expanded nationwide. Hence, and because of the paucity of previous research as mentioned above, we are not able to provide a description of how SBM practices may have changed over time.

CHAPTER THREE

Status of School-Based Management Implementation

This chapter describes how SBM is currently practiced in Indonesia. The chapter draws on data from the surveys and case studies. The first section discusses the extent to which schools have put in place the committee managerial structure required by central government directives. The extent to which schools perceive that they actually have the autonomy that was intended to be devolved to them is discussed in the second section. The third section focuses on whether the various local stakeholders fully participate in school decisions and the influence they have on these decisions. The next section assesses parental participation and voice in school affairs. A fifth section describes how schools are held accountable and by whom and whether schools inform stakeholders of their decisions as expected by central government directives. A summary is provided in the last section.

School Managerial Structure

To support SBM and encourage broad stakeholder participation, central government directives require that schools establish an SC and a BOS team and give guidance as to their sizes and memberships. They also require that schools involve a teaching board in the approval of the school's midterm and annual plans. Beyond these requirements, principals, as the equivalent of the chief executive officer of the school, may establish other committees to assist them in the management of the school. The extent to which they do so may indicate their desire to maximize participation of stakeholders in school affairs.

An SBM Managerial Structure Was Reported to Be in Place in a Majority of Schools

The majority of schools established all committees expected by central government directives and some schools added other special purpose committees as well. As required, the majority of schools (98 percent) had a school committee in 2010. About two-thirds of schools and half of schools had established a BOS team and a teaching board, respectively, also as required (Figure 3.1). In addition, a significant share of schools established a working group of teachers to help prepare the four-year plan (65 percent), an SBM team (54 percent), and a school budget team (37 percent). However, the extent to which these various committees were actually operational was not always certain. In our case study, 27 of the 40 sampled schools had indicated in response to our survey that they had an SBM team. However, when in the case study we asked to interview its members, all but one school said that they actually did not have such a team. In addition, the membership of the BOS team was often said to be made up of just the principal and a "treasurer" teacher picked by the principal to fulfill the BOS program's required administrative tasks. This suggests that some of these committees were either not operative or involved minimal actual participation of stakeholders.

About 11 percent of schools reported that they had established all six types of committees. Another 12 percent established five of the six types of committees, excluding a budget committee. The remaining schools had various combinations of these committees.

Parents Dominated the School Committees

The size of school committees averaged 8.3 members, about equal to the minimum size of nine members suggested by central government directives. Across the nation, parents accounted for about three-quarters of SC members, community and village council representatives accounted for about 20 percent, and teachers the remaining 4 or so percent (Figure 3.2). However, many of the parents indicated

Figure 3.1
Percentage of Schools with Selected Committees, by Type of Committee, 2010

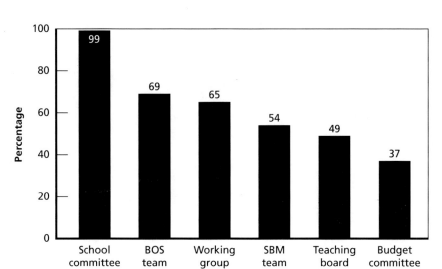

SOURCE: World Bank SBM National Survey (2010), principal and teacher surveys.
NOTES: N = 397–400 principals and 2,352 teachers. A school was deemed to have a working group or teaching board if the majority of up to six of its teachers surveyed responded as having one.
RAND *MG1229-3.1*

that they also had other functions, so that the representation of other stakeholders was greater than suggested above. For instance, 11 percent of parents also reported being community members, such as religious leaders or NGO representatives, and another 2 percent were also on the village or city council.

The backgrounds of the SC chairs were generally similar to that of the membership with a slightly higher representation of community representatives (Figure 3.2).

As suggested above, not all types of stakeholders were represented on the school committees of all schools. Whereas 98 percent of schools had parents on their school committee, only 69 percent had representation from teachers, and about half had representation from the village or city council (Table 3.1, second column). The principal was a member of the SC in 10 percent of schools.

Figure 3.2
Percentage of School Committee Chairs and Members, by Background and How Selected, 2010

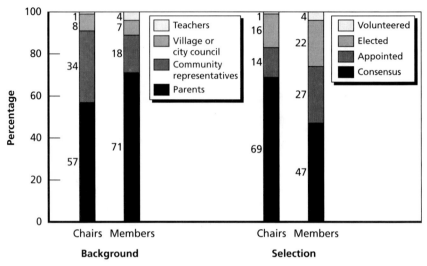

SOURCE: World Bank SBM National Survey (2010), SC chair and member surveys.
NOTE: N = 393 SC chairs and 388 members.
RAND *MG1229-3.2*

Apart from their majority presence on nearly all school committees, parents were less likely to be represented on other school teams. Parents were represented in about one-third of BOS teams, in spite of the directive that one parent be included on the school's BOS team, and in about 50 percent of the SBM teams and budget committees (Table 3.1). Unlike the school committees, these other school teams were typically headed by the principal and nearly always were said to include a teacher and an SC member, consistent with the expectations that these two types of school stakeholders be involved in school affairs.

Selection of School Committee Members Was Not Transparent

More attention needs to be given to the selection of SC chairs and members to ensure that the process is transparent and democratic, as expected by central government directives. Overall, 16 percent of chairs

Table 3.1
Percentage of Schools, by Type of Committee Member Representation in Selected Committees

Committee Member	School Committee	BOS Team	Management Team	Budget Committee
Principal	10	95	DA	95
Vice principal	DA	21	28	22
Teacher	69	97	99	96
SC member	NA	86	88	86
Parent[a]	98	35	55	43
Educational representative	16	DA	DA	DA
Village or city council	42	DA	DA	DA
Community representative	56	62	62	59

SOURCE: World Bank SBM National Survey (2010), principal survey.

NOTES: N = 147–400 principals. "DA" means "did not ask."

[a]For BOS management and budget committees, the parent may not also serve on the SC.

and less than 25 percent of SC members were said to have been elected (Figure 3.2). The primary form of selection of SC chairs and members in 2010 was by consensus and secondarily by appointment, typically by the principal. There were no major differences in these prevailing modes of selection among parents, teachers, community representatives, and village or city council representatives. SC members in rural areas were more likely to have volunteered, whereas those in urban areas were more likely to have been chosen by consensus.

In focus groups, SC members said that communication or social skills and willingness to serve were the typical backgrounds of the serving members. In a few instances, the key position of treasurer or secretary was given to a teacher, although not necessarily one teaching in the school. The selection of SC members was reported by focus group participants to be done every three to five years.

Interactions Between Principals and District Staff Were Frequent

The frequency of meetings held by teams and committees on their own and with other stakeholders, including school principals, is one indicator of their level of involvement in school affairs.

Principals met most frequently with the district staff and their teaching board, on average once a month over the school year 2009–2010, suggesting that consultations among these three stakeholders were routine (Figure 3.3). It also suggests the continuing dependence of principals on district input and oversight as we discuss in more detail in the next section. The frequency of these meetings did not differ between urban and rural areas.

Meetings of committees on their own or with other school teams were relatively rare. The BOS teams met on their own quarterly, and SC chairs reported meeting with their principal on average 2.5 times in the previous year. By themselves, SC members reported that they met from zero to three times a year, averaging 1.5 times in the previous

Figure 3.3
Number of Meetings in the Previous Year Between Selected Stakeholders, 2010

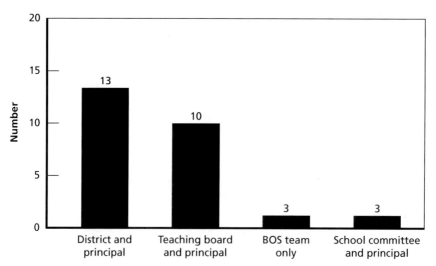

SOURCE: World Bank SBM National Survey (2010), principal survey.
NOTE: N = 281–400 principals.
RAND MG1229-3.3

year. Typically, SC members would meet at key school events to which all parents were also invited, such as at the beginning of the school year, at the distribution of the student grade reports, or at the end of the year. SC focus group participants said that meetings between the principal and the full SC were rare and took place only when called by the principal.

Autonomy

Perceived School Autonomy Was High
Consistent with the SBM concept, principals reported that they enjoyed a high level of autonomy in making decisions about their school's personnel, pedagogy and instruction, and budget allocation. On average, 90 percent of principals reported that they had decisionmaking authority in 11 areas of school operations, including teacher recruitment and hiring, setting the school vision and curriculum, selecting textbooks and teaching materials, and allocating the school budget (Figure 3.4).

Given that the central government has the authority to assign teachers to schools, the autonomy perceived by principals in the area of teacher recruitment and hiring was unexpected. One potential explanation is that principals were referring to the recruitment and hiring of non-PNS teachers (i.e., those not paid and assigned by the central government).[1] Eighty-eight percent of schools had teachers hired locally as non-PNS teachers using BOS funds. Nationwide, about one-third of elementary school teachers were non-PNS. It is also possible that principals had opportunities to negotiate with the central government, through their districts, the assignments of specific teachers to their schools.

Even though principals are responsible for the management of their schools, they rarely made decisions independently. In any one area, only 11 to 29 percent of principals reported making school-related decisions without the participation of other stakeholders (Figure 3.5). They more frequently made decisions alone in defining the school

---

[1]   The question did not specify the type of teachers.

Figure 3.4
Percentage of Principals Reporting That They Had Decisionmaking
Authority, by Type of Decision, 2010

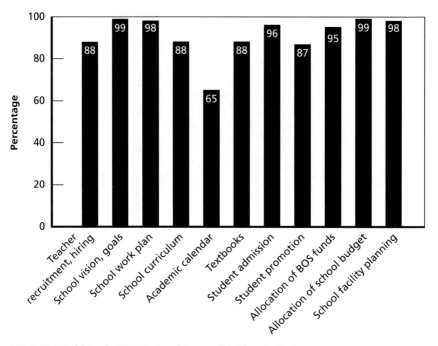

SOURCE: World Bank SBM National Survey (2010), principal survey.
NOTE: N = 400 principals.
RAND MG1229-3.4

vision and goals, school work plan, and teacher recruitment and hiring. Principals in rural areas were more likely than their urban counterparts to make independent decisions on non-PNS teacher hiring, student admission, and allocation of BOS funds.

Stakeholder Participation

Schools Made Decisions by Consensus of Varying Stakeholders

As reported by principals, school operational decisions typically were made by consensus of the principals and varying combinations of stakeholders, although rarely with the active participation of SC mem-

Figure 3.5
Percentage of Principals Reporting That They Solely Have Made Final
Decisions, by Type of Decision, 2010

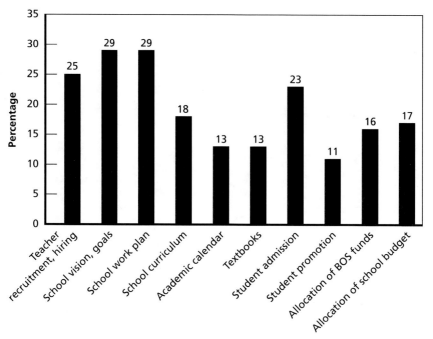

SOURCE: World Bank SBM National Survey (2010), principal survey.
NOTE: N = 400 principals.
RAND MG1229-3.5

bers. On average, in only about 22 percent of schools were final decisions (over ten different school operations[2]) made by the principal only
(Figure 3.6).

In another 22 percent of schools, decisions were said to be made
by the combined trio of the principal, teachers, and the SC. This trio
was the most likely to make "joint" decisions about the allocation
of BOS funds, the school budget, and developing the school's work
plan. However, as discussed further below, SC participation actually
meant informing the chair of the committee rather than having active

---

[2] Excluding the academic calendar, which was most frequently set by the district without
school input.

Figure 3.6
Percentage of Schools, by Stakeholders Participating in Decisions
Across Ten School Matters, 2010

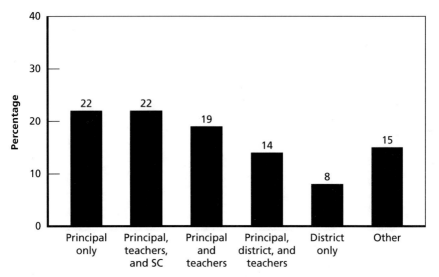

SOURCE: World Bank SBM National Survey (2010), principal survey.
NOTES: N = 400 principals. Average percentages of decisions made over ten school matters.
RAND *MG1229-3.6*

participation of the committee chair and its members. Teachers joined the principals in making decisions in 19 percent of schools—they were most likely to participate in decisions on the school's vision, mission, and goals and on the school's work plan.

Overall, in nearly two out of three schools, decisions were reportedly made without involvement of the SC, district, or other governmental education agencies. In about 14 percent of schools, decisions were made by the principal and the district, with involvement of teachers; in another 8 percent of schools, decisions were made solely by the district.

The tendency of principals to involve others in sharing decision-making was supported by both teachers and SC members. Nearly all (94 percent) of surveyed SC chairs agreed that the principal of their school relied on consensus for decisionmaking. Similarly, most surveyed teachers (96 percent) agreed that their principal had established teams for sharing leadership in their school. This is also consistent with the comments elicited in the case study. Asked whether they needed approval from any stakeholders from within or outside the school to make changes in the school's goals and mission, academic schedule, budget, textbooks used in the classroom, or the annual plan, most principals responded by describing who they consulted with or informed of decisions made. They often emphasized that they never decided on an issue by themselves, in some cases out of fear of making a wrong decision or of being perceived as being arrogant or authoritarian:

> My authority is limited in this office. Here I just manage, we are all friends. These friends [teachers] implement the programs, not me.

> If anything happened, we discuss it with teachers, along with the committee, and then we ask for supervisor's instructions, so we don't decide by ourselves.

Teacher Participation in Decisions Was Reportedly High

After principals, *teachers or the teaching board* were the stakeholders most frequently reported as participating in making school operational decisions, being involved on the average (across ten different school operations) in 65 percent of schools (Figure 3.7). According to principals, they were most involved in decisions regarding classroom instructional issues, including student promotion and textbook selection. The majority of teachers interviewed for the case study tended to agree that they actively participated in most, if not all, key decisions in their schools. Decisions in which they were the least likely to participate were in the choice of non-PNS staff. These teachers reported meeting with their principals monthly or even more frequently, as was noted above. At the same time, in a minority of schools the teacher focus group members reported that teachers were rarely involved in making most decisions in their school. These teachers described their principal as semi-authoritarian to simply authoritarian.

Apart from their involvement in school decisionmaking, teachers in the case study reported having a great deal of autonomy in their classrooms, although the degree of autonomy differed depending on

Figure 3.7
Percentage of Schools in Which Stakeholders Participated in Decisions Across Ten School Matters, by Type of Stakeholder, 2010

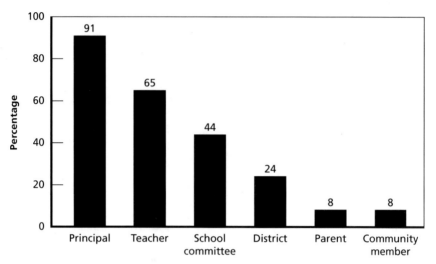

SOURCE: World Bank SBM National Survey (2010), principal survey.
NOTE: N = 400 principals.
RAND MG1229-3.7

the classroom practice. All teachers said that they needed no approval from anyone to make changes in their instructional methods or in the way they grouped students in the classroom. Most also said that they did not need approval to change the sequence in which they taught the curriculum, although a significant minority (one-third of teacher focus group participants) said that they "were not allowed" to make such a change, as the curriculum was set by the "authorities."

With regard to making changes in which textbooks to use in the classroom, most teachers in the focus groups said that only their principal's approval was needed as long as the books selected were consistent with the curriculum content. Principal approval was needed because it involved using BOS funds to buy the books. Some teachers in the focus groups also indicated that they needed approval from their "cluster of schools," because schools within a subdistrict were "required" to use the same textbooks.

The decisionmaking process to determine which students should be retained was described in the same way across case study schools.

It started with the classroom teacher identifying the students they wanted to retain. It was followed by an all-teacher meeting with the principal to discuss and make a decision on each individual case, which in part depended on the number of students who were recommended to be retained in the first place. In some schools, parents might also be consulted.

Many case study principals said that they also consulted with other principals and teachers in the cluster of schools in their subdistrict before making decisions:

> Obviously we talk to other principals and schools; we don't dare go on our own.

School Committee Participation in Decisionmaking Was Low

Deferential attitudes toward school staff, insufficient knowledge of school affairs, lack of time, and principals' narrow views of the role of the school committee reportedly prevented school committees from participating in school affairs to the extent anticipated by SBM governmental directives.

Principals reported that the SC participated in final decisions in an average of 44 percent of schools (Figure 3.7). They were most likely said, as previous studies have found, to be involved in matters other than pedagogy and instruction, including school facility planning and the allocation of the school's budget and BOS funds. They were least likely to be among decisionmakers in the selection of textbooks and the curriculum.

However, case study data indicate that principals' reports of SC participation may be overestimated. In focus groups, SC chairs and members said that they were minimally involved in school affairs. In describing their involvement, they used such phrases as "don't get involved really," "don't interfere," "don't want to be proactive," "only for support," and "not active." In the words of a few SC respondents:

> If the school committee is involved in aspects other than infrastructure, it instills the perception that we don't trust teachers.

> We wait for the invitation from the school principal. If there is no invitation, we just do nothing.

> We don't understand about school problems, they [teachers and principal] understand them better, so we leave everything to the school.

> We have never given any suggestion, as we are Javanese; we just follow the higher authority.

> Teachers should feel comfortable, not supervised by the school committee, so it [SC] must limit involvement. Eastern culture thinks that being supervised is annoying.

In particular, SC members were not actively involved in three important ways. First, their involvement in the allocation of BOS funds was pro forma, even though the BOS program provides for an active role of the SC. In the focus groups, both BOS team and SC focus group members generally agreed that SC members were rarely, if ever, actively involved or consulted in making BOS fund allocations. The common pattern was that the principal and treasurer, along with the teacher council or selected teachers, would make the allocation. Once completed, the document would be given to the SC chair for signature as is required by central government directives. Not one school suggested that the SC chair ever asked for changes in the allocations made by the school.

A similar pattern of nonparticipation of SC members in the preparation of the annual plan was reported in the case studies by both principals and SC members. SC members were not involved in preparing the annual working plan in about two-thirds of the case study schools, and in the remaining case study schools, the SC chair was just generally informed about the plan. By contrast, teachers were nearly always said to be involved in the preparation of the annual plan.

Finally, in all SC case study focus groups except one, participants indicated that the committee did not get involved in the teaching and learning process.

In addition to the reason implied in the quotations from SC members listed above, other reasons mentioned by SC members and principals for SC noninvolvement in school decisions included insufficient capacity and knowledge and lack of time. Most parents and other SC members are reportedly too busy working, especially in rural areas, to be able to come to school for meetings during the day and so, if principals communicate with the SC at all, it is exclusively with the SC chair:

> The SC members are busy in the working hours. It is enough to have consultations with teachers.

> School committee members, they are ignorant and they don't want to know. As long as the school is good, run smoothly, and nothing happens, they are okay.

> The school committee is also involved. We don't want to make them stepchildren. But, we want them to only know, listen, and they can appraise.

This is not to say that SCs were not thought to be useful in many ways, even though they are not as broadly or deeply involved as envisioned by SBM. Many SCs in the case studies were engaged in small projects related to upgrading the school infrastructure, such as adding a fence around the school to increase student safety, upgrading bathrooms or building water containers to improve hygiene, fixing roof leaks, paving the school yard, or bringing in flowers to decorate the school and make it more pleasant.

SC members mainly saw themselves (as did principals) as intermediaries or the bridge between the school and parents when the principal needed to communicate with parents or needed something from them. They also saw themselves as cheerleaders to encourage parents to make their children study harder. In particular, an important role most SCs reported playing was gathering sixth-grade parents to inform them of the school's plans to prepare their children for the national exam, impress on them the importance of this exam for their children and the school's reputation, and encourage them to take an active part by monitoring their children's play and television time at home:

> We also give suggestion or motivation to parents, such as please help the children study more because they face the exam.

At many of the schools, SC focus group participants were vocal about students' lack of discipline about studying, and they saw as part of their jobs encouraging parents to pay more attention to their children's studies. Also, they complained about the lack of discipline on the part of teachers who frequently arrived late or left early.

When asked whether the SCs could be more useful in helping to improve their schools, few of the case study SC respondents volunteered activities that they could undertake in addition to what they were already engaged in.

Districts Maintained a High Level of Influence

Although surveyed principals said that their district was not heavily involved in making decisions on matters affecting their school, they also said that they continued to depend on their district for guidance in most areas.

In about one-quarter of schools, principals stated that their district participated in decisions on their school's matters (Figure 3.7), being most often involved in setting the school curriculum, teacher management, selecting textbooks, and defining the school calendar. The district was the sole decisionmaker of the school calendar in one-third of schools. At the same time, districts were said to maintain a high level of influence over school decisions, seemingly consistent with the consensus approach to decisionmaking preferred by a majority of principals. Most striking was the relatively high influence that districts reportedly had over schools' missions and priorities.

Districts' self-reported level of influence on various school matters was equivalent to the self-reported influence of principals on the same school matters, including defining the school vision, developing the annual school plan, setting the school calendar, and determining the content of staff development—both averaging a score of 3.2 to 3.6 on a scale of 4.0, indicating that they were both "somewhat to very influential" in these areas (Table 3.2). The equivalency of influence that districts and principals had on these school matters was confirmed by the ratings of principals on these matters.[3]

---

[3] Principal average ratings (on a scale of 4.0) of district influence were 3.1 in teacher assignment, 3.0 on developing the school plan, and 3.1 on determining the content of staff development. They were lower for district influence on selection of textbooks and school budget allocation (both 2.6).

Table 3.2
Average Influence Ratings, by Type of Stakeholder, 2010

Type of School Decision	Principal	SC Chair	Teacher	District	Parent
Personnel management					
Hire, fire PNS teachers	DA	2.2	DA	2.9	DA
Assign teachers to school	DA	DA	DA	3.6	DA
Evaluate teachers	DA	2.0	DA	3.5	DA
Hire, fire non-PNS teachers	3.1	DA	DA	DA	DA
Pedagogy/instruction					
Set school vision	3.3	2.2	2.8	3.2	1.8
Draft school plan	3.4	2.2	2.8	3.0	1.4
Set instruction time for academic subject	DA	DA	DA	3.1	DA
Determine school calendar	3.2	1.5	DA	3.3	1.2
Select methods of instruction	DA	DA	3.2	2.7	DA
Select textbooks	3.2	1.5	3.2	2.2	1.3
Determine syllabi	3.2	DA	3.1	2.7	DA
Assess student performance	DA	DA	DA	1.9	DA
Determine staff development	3.3	DA	2.9	3.6	DA
Set student admission criteria	3.4	2.2	DA	DA	DA
Develop curriculum	DA	1.6	DA	DA	1.2
Develop student tests	DA	DA	3.2	DA	DA
Budget					
Allocate school budget	3.4	2.2	2.8	2.4	1.4
Purchase supplies	3.3	DA	DA	1.7	DA
Allocate BOS funds	3.4	2.4	2.8	DA	1.4
Plan school facility	3.3	2.6	DA	DA	DA
Community-school relationship	DA	2.6	DA	DA	DA

SOURCE: World Bank SBM National Survey (2010), principal, SC chair, teacher, district, and parent surveys.

NOTES: N = 400 principals, 393 SC chairs, 2,352 teachers, 54 heads of district, and 1,518 parents. The scale was 1 = not influential, 2 = a little influential, 3 = somewhat influential, 4 =very influential. "DA" means "did not ask."

By contrast, district-level respondents reported having "little to some influence" (average score of 2.7 or lower on a scale of 4.0) in making instructional decisions, such as choosing textbooks and teaching materials and determining lesson content and syllabi. They also reported having even less influence on the allocation of the school budget and the purchasing of supplies.

Underlining the continuing high influence of districts on school matters, their influence was rated higher than that of teachers on developing the school vision, developing the school annual plan, and determining the content of staff development. However, as one would expect, teachers rated their influence as higher than that of districts (but not higher than principals) on such instructional matters as the selection of instructional methods, selection of textbooks, determination of lesson content and syllabi, and the development of student achievement tests (scores 3.1 to 3.2).

The continuing influence of districts on schools' policies and practices was confirmed by the principals interviewed in the case study. Asked if there were areas of school policy or practices that they wished their district did not get involved with, principals were unanimous in indicating that not only were there no such areas, but that most welcomed their dependence on district guidance. As expressed by various principals:

> We need the assistance of the district, like thoughts and directions. We cannot stand for ourselves; we still need to be guided in all aspects.

> We are inseparable from the education office because this office is our superintendent. Every time we have a problem, we must consult with the office. We defer to them always.

> No, because I realize I would not be able to do it by myself; I still need the support and guidance from the district.

> We, as the implementer of the policies from higher authority, if we make a policy our self, it will break the rules.

Yes, the department is like our own parents; therefore, we always need their guidance.

Now, all matters are regulated by district, from attendance, discipline, working discipline, uniform discipline.

When asked who they would consult with for making changes to their school's curriculum, nearly half of principals in the case study schools indicated that, should they do so, they would consult with officials at the subdistrict or district levels:

The structure from the bottom to top is school, supervisor, head of elementary school affairs, head of districts. Whatever the issues faced by the school, either in the process, composing the program or implementation, that's the structure.

Still, a few of our case study principals would prefer to have less interference from their district:

If I could choose, I would rather not involve the district. We can use our own teaching methods to encourage students' creativity.

I think in fund expenditures, DINAS [Ministry of National Education] should not to be too involved. We have school autonomy, so don't press too hard.

Unlike districts whose relatively high influence on school decisions significantly outweighed their reportedly (by principals) low participation in school decisions, the low influence of school committees tracked closely with their reported low or nonparticipation in school decisions. SC members' self-rated influence was highest for facility planning, fostering community-school relations, and allocating BOS resources, averaging 2.4 to 2.6 on a scale of 4.0. They were lowest in influence regarding such classroom instructional issues as curriculum, selection of textbooks, and evaluating teachers (1.5 to 2.0, or not influential to a little influential) (see Table 3.2).

Parental Voice and Involvement

Parents Had a Small Voice in School Matters

Parents' deferential attitudes toward school staff, perceptions of effective division of labor between school and home, and schools' lack of outreach appear to prevent parents from effectively exercising their voice in school affairs.

Parents were rarely part of final decisions on school matters, reportedly participating on the average in just 8 percent of schools (Figure 3.7). Indeed, parents themselves reported having little influence over a variety of school decisions (average score of 1.2 to 1.8) (Table 3.2). Setting the school vision was the area in which they reported having the highest influence (1.8), whereas the area they rated as having the lowest influence in was the curriculum (1.2).

Also, only one in every four principals on average (across 11 different school matters) reported that they had received any input from parents. They most frequently received input from parents in setting the school's vision and developing the school's annual plan (44 percent of principals), planning for facility improvements (39 percent), and allocating school budget (38 percent) (Figure 3.8). However, even this level of participation may be overestimated by principals. From 83 to 91 percent of parents surveyed reported that they never provided input on school budget, helped raise funds, served on a committee, or volunteered in school (Figure 3.9).

Interactions between teachers and parents were also said to be minimal. With few exceptions, case study teachers said that they never contacted parents. In turn, few parents said that they ever contacted teachers outside the report card distribution day. They would typically meet with their child's teacher only if invited by him or her. The prevailing attitude seems to be best captured by these parents' statements:

> At school, children are the teachers' responsibilities, at home the parents'.

> It is best that parents don't interfere at the school. If there is a problem, it is the teacher/school responsibility to let the parents know.

Figure 3.8
Percentage of Principals Reporting That Parents Provided Input, by Type of Input, 2010

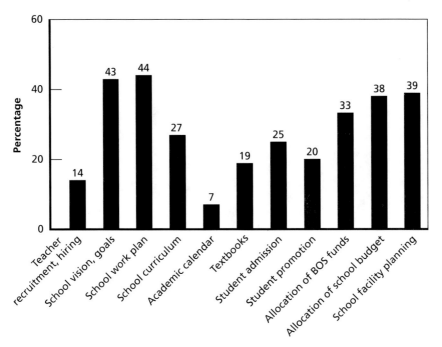

SOURCE: World Bank SBM National Survey (2010), principal survey.
NOTE: N = 400 principals.
RAND MG1229-3.8

Schools themselves did not appear to encourage parent participation in school matters. The majority of case study principals said that they did not hold formal meetings with parents, although they might invite individual parents to discuss student performance or attendance issues. They said that they "met" parents twice a year when the latter picked up their child's report card. At that time, principals might inform them about school activities and receive parents' comments and suggestions. It is thus not surprising that, although a majority of parents surveyed (60 percent) reported that they had attended school meetings in the previous two years, less than 20 percent reported that the school's vision, annual plan, curriculum, or extracurricular activities were discussed at these meetings (Figure 3.10).

Figure 3.9
Percentage of Parents Participating in School Activities, by Type of Activity, 2010

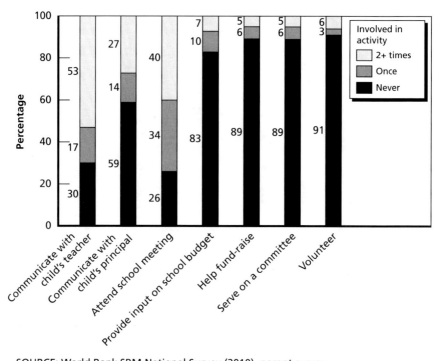

SOURCE: World Bank SBM National Survey (2010), parent survey.
NOTE: N = 2,400 parents.
RAND MG1229-3.9

As noted above, not even school committees—at least at the present—offered an avenue for providing parents with information on school activities, let alone accepting parental input and influence. Case study SC members said that they never held a meeting with parents to elicit their opinions about the school or even to inform them of school activities:

> When they get an invitation, they would be reluctant to come since they [the parents] have a lot to do.

> Frankly, there is no activity of the SC without the participation of the headmaster's invitation.

Figure 3.10
Percentage of Parents Reporting That They Attended School Meetings, by School Matter Discussed, 2010

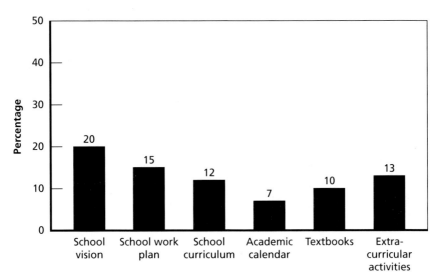

SOURCE: World Bank SBM National Survey (2010), parent survey.
NOTE: N = 2,400 parents.
RAND *MG1229-3.10*

> The meeting between parents and the SC is no longer held because students don't pay tuition, even though BOS is managed by the school.

Nearly half of surveyed parents did not know that their school had an SC, and 30 percent more had never attended an SC meeting or received information from their SC. Parents said that they were informed of school activities mainly through their children. Teachers tell the students about forthcoming events or things to be brought to school the next day and the children, in turn, tell their parents.

Minimal Parental and Community Pressure to Improve Education

The result of low SC and parental active participation, or even presence, in school matters is that the majority of educational staff, from principals to teachers and district staff, felt no to little pressure to improve student performance from either parents or the community at large. Teachers, although being the most likely to interact with parents, were the least likely to feel pressure from parents or the community to improve student achievement (Table 3.3). By contrast, the most likely to feel any pressure from parents or the community were the heads of district supervisors. It is the role of district supervisors to monitor school performance and help improve it.

Principals, district and subdistrict heads, and education board chairs fell in between the two extremes, feeling between "very weak" and "weak" pressure from parents and the community.

Parents' high level of satisfaction with interactions with their children's schools may be contributing to the lack of pressure for improvements felt primarily by education sector stakeholders. More than 90 percent of parents "agreed" or "strongly agreed" that their child's school provided opportunities for parents to file complaints, that the principal was responsive to parents' opinions and feedback on school-related issues, and that teachers were responsive to their opinions and feedback regarding their child's education.

Table 3.3
Percentage of Stakeholders Reporting Pressure from Parents and the Community to Improve Student Achievement, by Type of Stakeholder, 2010

Stakeholder	Parent		Community	
	No Pressure	Pressure Score	No Pressure	Pressure Score
District head	37	1.6	39	1.7
Subdistrict head	45	1.7	59	1.3
Supervisor head	24	2.2	26	2.0
Education board chair	42	1.5	44	1.5
Principal	37	1.7	48	1.4
Teacher	57	1.1	65	0.9

SOURCE: World Bank SBM National Survey (2010), all surveys.

NOTES: N = 400 principals, 2,353 teachers, 54 district heads, 47 subdistrict heads, 54 heads of supervisors, and 52 education board chairs. The pressure score is based on scale of 0 to 4 with 0 = no pressure, 1 = very weak pressure, 2 = weak pressure, 3 = intense pressure, and 4 = very intense pressure.

Parents Did Not Take Advantage of Parental Choice

Finally, few parents took advantage of the choice they had in selecting a school for their children. Although 80 percent of parents indicated that there was more than one school to choose from in their village or urban area, only 8 percent of parents reported applying to more than one school (Figure 3.11).

One of the main reasons for not taking advantage of school choice was accessibility and possibly inertia on the part of parents. It is likely that parents were unaware that they could choose the school they wanted their child to attend, just as many had never heard of school committees. It is also possible that SBM had not yet resulted in diversity of quality and type of academic offerings, at least at the primary school level, to offer much choice. Furthermore, parents received no information (other than perhaps by word of mouth) upon which to make informed school choices. For instance, they did not receive information on student performance or school programs in schools in their

Figure 3.11
Percentage of Parents Who Had School Choice Options and Applied to Two or More Schools, 2010

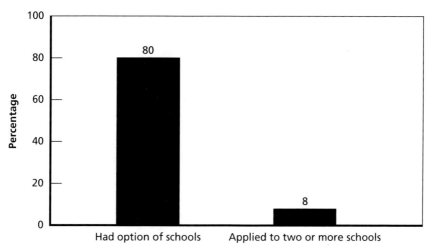

SOURCE: World Bank SBM National Survey (2010), parent survey.
NOTE: N = 2,400 parents.
RAND MG1229-3.11

community that would have enabled them to make choices based on school quality and offerings.

Accountability and Transparency

Although SBM places school academic and management decisions in the hands of school staff and stakeholders, it also places increased oversight and monitoring responsibilities over these decisions on education districts, school committees, parents, and the immediate community. Governmental directives on SBM require that information on student performance, BOS allocation and budget, and other decisions be communicated to these various stakeholders.

District Supervisors Monitored Schools Frequently

Districts said that they were very involved in monitoring the activities of their schools, although the extent to which this monitoring resulted in ongoing corrective actions was not gauged. According to surveyed district heads, an average of about 8 percent of their workforce was dedicated to monitoring school financial performance, with about half of districts reporting having no staff monitoring school financial performance. In turn, district supervisors monitored school administration, principals, and teachers on an ongoing basis. On average, one supervisor was assigned for every 13 elementary schools. Ninety percent of surveyed districts said that supervisors were to visit each of their assigned schools about monthly. Surveyed principals, however, reported less frequent supervisor visits to their individual schools. About 40 percent of principals reported that visits by supervisors were quarterly or less frequent (Figure 3.12). There were no significant variations in frequency of supervisor visits between urban and rural schools.

District staff other than supervisors rarely visited schools. A majority of principals (78 percent) reported that district staff visited their schools two or fewer times a year, with nearly 40 percent of principals reporting having not been visited by other district staff during the past year (Figure 3.12).

Figure 3.12
Percentage of Districts and Schools, by Frequency of Monitoring Visits Made or Received and Type of Monitoring Staff, 2010

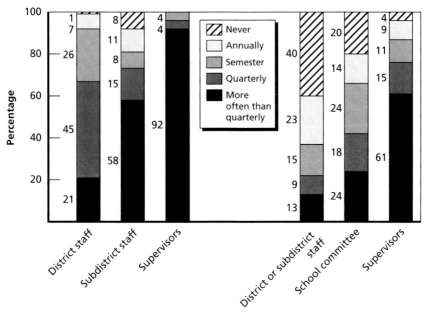

Reported by district   Reported by principal

SOURCE: World Bank SBM National Survey (2010), principal, district head, subdistrict head, and head of supervisor surveys.
NOTE: N = 400 principals and 47–54 staff district heads, subdistrict heads, and heads of supervisors. District staff visits were reported by the heads of districts, visits by supervisors were reported by the heads of supervisors, and visits by subdistrict staff were reported by subdistrict heads.
RAND MG1229-3.12

SC members were said by surveyed principals to "visit schools for monitoring purposes" quarterly on average. This is equivalent to the frequency at which the use of BOS funds is to be reported, suggesting that it simply means that the SC chair was informed and asked to sign the BOS forms at those times as discussed above. About 20 percent of schools reported receiving no monitoring visits by their SC.

Monitoring of BOS. Nearly half of surveyed districts reported that district staff monitored BOS on a quarterly basis, with another 29 percent reporting being monitoring even more frequently. This frequency of BOS monitoring visits by district staff differed only slightly from the frequency reported by surveyed principals. More than half of principals reported quarterly or more frequent BOS monitoring visits by district staff (Figure 3.13).

Principals reported that SC members monitored BOS nearly as frequently as district staff, again suggesting, as above, that they did so when they were required by BOS guidelines to approve (sign) the school's allocation of BOS. This pattern of BOS monitoring by both district staff and SC chairs suggests that "monitoring" was more likely to mean checking that all appropriate forms were properly and accurately filled out.

Purposes of Monitoring. Monitoring duties by supervisors and district staff were said to range from providing feedback on principal and teacher performance to checking on the conditions of school facilities, monitoring or observing classrooms and instruction, assessing teacher training needs, and reviewing and approving the school budget (Figure 3.14). There appears to have been minimal division of

Figure 3.13
Percentage of Districts and Schools, by Frequency of BOS Fund Monitoring and Type of Monitoring Staff, 2010

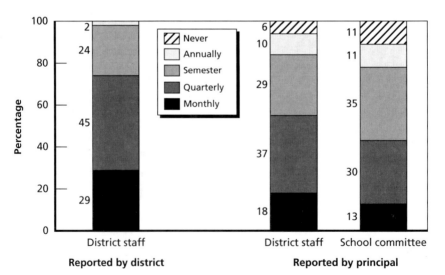

SOURCE: World Bank SBM National Survey (2010), principal and district head surveys.
NOTE: N = 396 principals and 54 district heads.
RAND MG1229-3.13

Figure 3.14
Percentage of Districts, by Purpose of Monitoring Visit and Type of Monitoring Staff, 2010

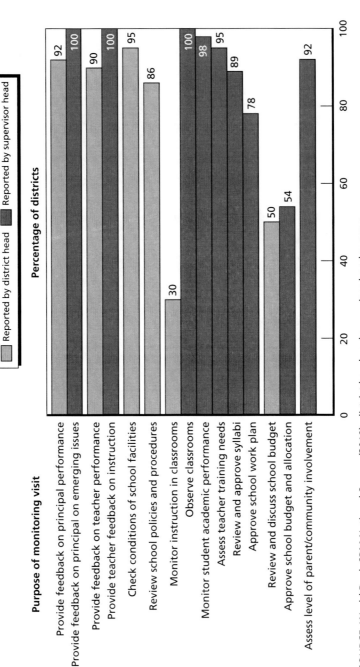

SOURCE: World Bank SBM National Survey (2010), district head and supervisor head surveys.
NOTES: N = 53 district heads and 54 heads of supervisors. Each type of respondent was asked to respond to a specific set of questions, as noted above.

RAND MG1229-3.14

labor between education district staff and supervisors in the type of activities monitored. The former were somewhat less likely to focus on classroom instruction, whereas the latter included these aspects in their monitoring. Otherwise, there appears to have been a great deal of overlap in the monitoring done by these two types of staff.

As described by case studies' principals and teachers, the typical supervisor visit consisted of checking that both school and classroom administrative reports, including teacher and student attendance and classroom profile reports, were correctly filled out. Supervisors also observed classrooms from anywhere between 15 minutes and one hour, focusing on teaching methods and the appropriate use of props by teachers. Upon completion of the visits, they were said to give principals and teachers feedback on administrative issues that needed correction and input to teachers who had "teaching technique deficiencies:"

> [The supervisor] observes the teacher's presentation to students in the classroom, classroom control, and they see whether we are making errors.

> [The supervisor] makes an assessment of how the teacher fills out the forms. If we have weaknesses, the supervisor will inform us. The supervisor also sees the attendance list and the learning implementation plan.

> The teacher is evaluated about the lesson plan and teaching method. The supervisor demonstrated directly how to teach PAKEM [active, creative, effective, and joyful learning] and we were asked not only to lecture, but also to practice it.

> They [supervisors] visit for administrative matters, such as RPP [learning implementation plan], how the teaching tools are used, and how we teach the class. They will give us suggestions.

> They observe how the teachers motivate students to learn, observe how students receive the lesson from teacher. . . . After the learning process, the supervisor provides direction, adds knowledge and corrects shortcomings.

When asked about what school improvements supervisors had asked them to make in their schools, case study principals identified three areas with about equal frequency: (1) Increase student achievement (in 40 percent of case study schools), (2) Increase teacher creativity or use of visual aids, and (3) Improve student or teacher discipline or attendance. This suggests that the focus of supervisory advice was more on *what* teachers ought to be doing and less on the more critical *how* they ought to do it. The continuing low level of student achievement and of parent and community involvement (in spite of districts' monitoring of the latter) may also suggest that there is little effective and sustained follow-up with improvement actions. To address these questions in the future, it will be important to collect information on the content of the monitoring actually taking place and the kind of follow-up actions that were taken to address identified issues.

Actions Taken with Underperforming Principals Were Mild

The majority of district heads (95 percent) reported they were responsible for evaluating the performance of principals. According to district heads, the criteria considered in evaluating principals were common to nearly all, including attendance, capacity and creativity, compliance with rules and procedures, student academic performance, and financial management. Also included as criteria, but in a smaller set of districts, were parental participation (80 percent of districts) and student dropout rate (78 percent).

About two-thirds of districts reported having underperforming principals. One common action taken by most districts with underperforming principals was reassignment, thereby most likely transferring the problem from one school to another. Another frequent action most districts took was to write a notification letter. About a third of districts with underperforming principals reported that they had demoted or fired an underperforming principal in the previous two years (Figure 3.15).

Teachers Did Not Receive Sufficient Feedback from Various Sources

Over 40 percent of teachers surveyed reported receiving no feedback from their principals and half reported receiving no feedback from

Figure 3.15
Percentage of Districts, by Type of Action Taken Against Underperforming
Principals, 2008–2010

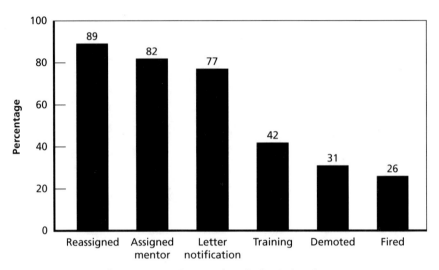

SOURCE: World Bank SBM National Survey (2010), district head survey.
NOTES: N = 28 district heads. Only district heads with underperforming principals over
the previous two years were asked to respond to this question.
RAND MG1229-3.15

supervisors. Other sources of feedback, such as from other teachers, SC members, or other district staff, were even rarer. For instance, less than 20 percent of teachers reported that SC members or district staff had provided feedback in the past year (Figure 3.16).

About half of principals reported spending half a day or less per week observing classroom instruction, with the other half spending between 5 and 12 hours a week.

Most principals (95 percent) reported that they had evaluated their teachers at least once in the previous year (2009–2010), with the average principal evaluating teachers on average five times a year.

About 15 percent of principals reported that they had underperforming teachers in their school in the previous year. The most frequent action taken by principals (98 percent) was to provide the teacher with notification of the problem. About one-half of principals took such additional actions as sending the underperforming teacher for profes-

Figure 3.16
Percentage of Teachers Receiving Feedback on Their Teaching, by
Frequency of Feedback and Type of Staff Providing It, 2010

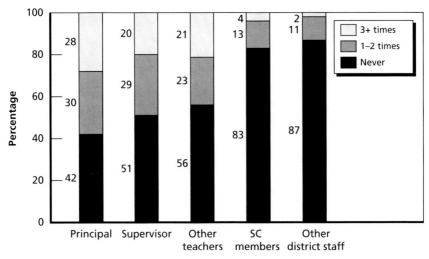

SOURCE: World Bank SBM National Survey (2010), teacher survey.
NOTE: N = 2,353 teachers. Only teachers who received any feedback were asked to
respond to this question.
RAND *MG1229-3.16*

sional development or assigning a teacher mentor. Fewer than one in
ten principals reported that an underperforming teacher had been fired
in the previous two years (Figure 3.17).

Information Provided to Parents Was Limited

Parental involvement in their child's school and in education more generally depends in part on the information they receive not only on the
performance of their children and the school but also on the school
facility and academic programs.

Overall, parents rarely were sent or received written information about their child's school, other than their child's report card.
About 30 percent of principals reported sending information about
their school's overall performance and a somewhat lower proportion
of parents indicated that they actually had received such information. A slightly higher proportion of schools sent and parents received

Figure 3.17
Percentage of Principals, by Action Taken with Underperforming Teachers, 2008–2010

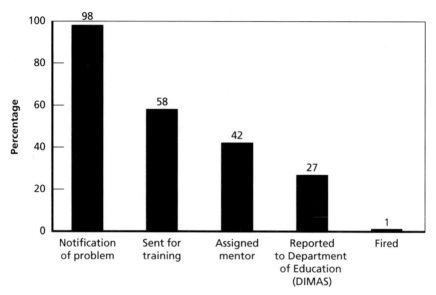

SOURCE: World Bank SBM National Survey (2010), principal survey.
NOTE: N = 60 principals. Only principals who had underperforming teachers were asked to respond to this question.
RAND *MG1229-3.17*

information on opportunities for parent involvement in the school (Figure 3.18).[4] Parents with children in urban schools were more likely than parents with children in rural schools to have received written information from their child's school.

The low share of schools that sent information and of parents who received information about the allocation of BOS funds[5] and about the

---

[4] Observers told us that information about school activities is mainly provided by word-of-mouth instead of in written form. Indeed, as noted above, children were the primary source of information for parents. It is unlikely that the information transmitted via schoolchildren pertains to anything other than extracurricular activities and items that children may be required to bring to school.

[5] Note, however, that information about BOS allocation of funds is only required to be posted on the school's bulletin board. In our visits to schools, even such posting was not a

Figure 3.18
Percentage of Principals Sending and of Parents Receiving Information, by Type of Information, 2010

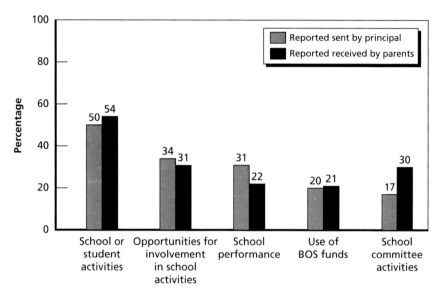

SOURCE: World Bank SBM National Survey (2010), principal and parent surveys.
NOTE: N = 400 principals and 2,400 parents.
RAND *MG1229-3.18*

activities of the SC is particularly telling, since it is mainly through these two latter mechanisms that parents might most effectively exercise their voice.

The main information that schools sent to parents and that parents said that they received in 2009–2010 was their child's report card. About half of parents received it at the end of each semester and 40 percent said that they had received it only once in the previous year (Figure 3.19).[6] About two-thirds of parents (61 percent) reported that the report card they received was somewhat easy to understand, and another 30 percent said it was very easy to understand.

---

widespread occurrence. This means of reporting was found to occur in 23 percent of schools by the *Independent Monitoring Report* (World Bank, 2011b).

[6] Since the survey data were collected in the spring of 2010, it is likely that most parents had not yet received the end-of-year report card for their child, so it is possible that most parents received a report card at least twice for the school year 2009–2010.

Figure 3.19
Percentage of Schools Sending and of Parents Receiving Student Report
Cards, by Frequency, 2010

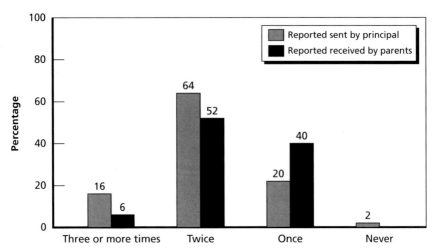

SOURCE: World Bank SBM National Survey (2010), principal and parent surveys.
NOTE: N = 400 principals and 2,400 parents.
RAND *MG1229-3.19*

Parents were not the only stakeholders who did not receive information about BOS allocation of funds by the school. Nearly one-third of SC chairs and members reported that they had not received this, even though the SC chair is expected to sign the allocation of BOS funds.

Another vehicle for expressing parental voice required by the central government is the school's designation of a staff member to receive parental complaints (Ministry of National Education, 2007). Less than half (44 percent) of principals reported having assigned a staff member to receive parental complaints.[7] About 18 percent of parents reported that they knew that their school had designated a staff member to receive complaints and respond to inquiries from the

---

[7] The *Independent Monitoring Report* found even fewer schools (16 percent) with a complaint unit (World Bank, 2011b). Our data are derived from the survey of principals, and the *Independent Monitoring Report* data were collected on-site and may be more accurate. This further suggests the tendency of survey respondents to provide somewhat more socially desirable answers than answers that actually reflect the practice.

community. About the same share of parents indicated that they had filed a complaint in the previous year. Among schools that assigned a staff member to take complaints, about half of the staff members were teachers and half were school administrators.

Summary

Most principals said that they put in place an administrative and decisionmaking structure to assist them in the management of their schools as required by central government directives. Nearly all schools had an SC that was made up primarily of parents and secondarily of teachers. Community-based and local government representation on these committees was low. SC members were typically selected "by consensus" or "appointment" rather than elected in a transparent and democratic way. Also, about two-thirds of schools had a BOS team and a teaching board. In addition, about half of schools reported establishing a school management team and one-third a school budget team.

However, our case study visits to schools suggest that some of these committees and teams were not operational. For instance, none of the 27 case study schools that responded to our surveys and said that they had an SBM team actually had one when asked to identify its members. Also, most BOS teams were said to involve only the principal and a treasurer teacher appointed by the principal and charged with mostly administrative duties. Similarly, most school committees indicated that they were mostly inactive, meeting about twice a year at "all-school" meetings and never meeting separately with parents. If principals interacted with the SC, it was nearly always with the SC chair only.

Principals and teachers reported that they benefited from a high level of autonomy in all key managerial and programmatic areas, including personnel, instruction, and allocation of available resources. On average, 90 percent of principals reported that they were involved in final decisions across 11 different school operational categories. Of note was the reported high autonomy of schools in the area of personnel hiring and assignment, even though the hiring and assignment of PNS teachers remained in the hands of the central government. One potential reason for this perception by principals is that nearly one-third of the nation's elementary school teaching staff is non-PNS and is hired locally by them using BOS or other discretionary funds. Another potential reason is that principals may be able to "negotiate" PNS teacher assignments with their districts with which they interact frequently. Similarly, teachers reported having a great deal of autonomy in the classroom, needing the approval of no one, including the principal, to change their instructional methods, groupings of students, and sequence of the curriculum. They felt more constrained in the choice of the main textbook, however.

Although principals were nearly always involved in making decisions in their schools, most also said that they rarely decided on an issue by themselves. The typical mode of decisionmaking at the school level was by consensus of varying combinations of stakeholders, with teachers most frequently participating in school decisions along with their principals (in two-thirds of schools). School committees were said by principals to be involved in school decisions in about one-third of schools. However, even this level of participation may be overestimated. In the case study focus groups, SC members were often emphatic that they were minimally involved in school affairs. Their attitude was one of no interference in school affairs and deference to principals and teachers. Even the SC's involvement in BOS fund allocation was said to be pro forma, with the SC chair asked to sign on after the allocation had been decided by the principal. Both principals and SC members agreed that this minimal involvement was in part due to two main factors: lack of availability of SC members during daytime and their lack of knowledge about school affairs.

This is not to say that school committees played no role at all. One role they played was to help schools communicate with and motivate parents of sixth-graders to make sure that their children attended additional classes to prepare for their final exams and to better monitor their study time. As for principals, they often said that they saw the SC mainly as an intermediary between the school and parents to inform parents about events in the school. However, parents indicated that they received information about the schools mainly from their children, not from the school committees.

Although districts were said by principals to rarely participate in making school decisions, they were said to continue to exercise a high level of influence. Their influence equaled or exceeded that of teachers across most managerial and programmatic areas, with the exception of classroom instructional matters. Principals interviewed in the case studies were unanimous in saying that they continued to need their district's guidance and that they rarely made a decision without discussing it with the district. The attitude of principals seemed to be guided by a fear of making a mistake or appearing to be too authoritarian.

Parental voice was reportedly minimal. The lack of effective parental input is due to several factors—some of parents' own making and some due to schools' lack of outreach and sharing of information. As with SC members, parents' attitude was one of noninterference in school affairs. They also were "satisfied" to "very satisfied" with their child's school. At the same time, schools rarely held parent meetings and rarely sent written information about school activities to parents other than their child's report card. The card contains no comparative information on schools in their area to enable parents to take advantage of school choice. In addition, nearly all SCs reported never meeting with parents to seek parental input. The net result was that principals and teachers reported feeling no or little pressure from parents and the community at large to improve school performance.

District accountability and monitoring of schools was said to be primarily done by district supervisors, who visited schools an average of five to six times a year, and subdistrict staff, who visited much less frequently. Reportedly, they checked the completeness of required school and classroom administrative reports, observed classrooms, monitored teacher performance, assessed teacher training needs, reviewed and approved the lesson syllabi, and monitored the allocation of BOS funds. At the conclusion of each visit, they gave principals and teachers feedback on any issues they may have identified. However, nearly half of teachers reported that they never received feedback from a supervisor, and the others said that they received some feedback one to three times a year. The feedback received was more in the form of *what* teachers should do than *how* they should do it.

Principals reported evaluating teachers once or more each year. About 15 percent of schools had underperforming teachers in the previous year. The most frequent actions taken by principals in these schools included written notifications or referrals to training. Rarely was the underperforming teacher fired. Two-thirds of districts reported that they had underperforming principals. Corrective actions taken by districts on underperforming principals consisted most frequently of reassignment to another school or writing a notification letter. About a third of districts reported that they had demoted or fired an underperforming principal in the previous two years.

CHAPTER FOUR

Capacity of Schools to Implement SBM

School and staff capacity, including monetary resources and principal, teacher, and other stakeholder knowledge and know-how, can be
expected to affect the way SBM is implemented, the extent to which
it is participatory, and how school academic and other decisions are
made. In this chapter, we look at the resources available to schools to
support SBM. We also discuss school stakeholders' understanding of
SBM and the preparedness of principals, teachers, and SC members to
implement SBM and make independent decisions.

Resources Available to Schools

In addition to funds received under the central government, schools
may receive BOS funds or aid from their provincial, district, and local
governments and from school fees or donations. Unlike the central
government's BOS program, which provides the same fixed amount
per student (Rp 397,000 per student per year in kabupatens and
Rp 400,000 per student per year in kotas) to all elementary schools, the
funds provided by provinces and districts may differ across these governmental entities, leading to broad variations in the amount schools
have available per student.

Central BOS Was the Primary Source of School Revenues

In 2009–2010 and nationwide, BOS accounted for about 83 percent of school discretionary[1] resources for the average school.[2] District BOS and aid accounted for another 9 percent and provincial BOS and aid another 5 percent. Monetary donations from school committees and parents were minimal and no fee revenues were reported by schools (Figure 4.1).

Some regions or districts within regions were more likely than others to provide resources additional to those provided by the central government's BOS program. Kalimantan and Sulawesi schools received relatively large contributions from provinces and districts: 28 and 19 percent of total revenues, respectively. At the other extreme, district revenues constituted only 3 percent of the average school's revenues in Maluku; however, those schools received 12 percent of their revenues from other sources, most likely from parental fees. Provinces provided a relatively large share of resources to schools in Sulawesi, whereas in the remaining regions, the districts provided more resources to their schools than did the provinces.

Schools in urban areas were also nearly four times more likely to receive additional funds from both their provinces and their districts (45 percent of school revenues) than were schools in rural areas (12 percent of school revenues).

---

[1]   Discretionary funds are funds that the schools can allocate at its discretion. See Chapter Two for details on the way school discretionary budgets were determined.

[2]   The 83 percent BOS program share of total school revenues represents the share for the "average school" obtained by computing the share of BOS in each school and then averaging across schools. Another view of the contribution of the BOS program to school finance can be obtained by adding all BOS and total funds across schools nationwide and then dividing the first by the second. This nationwide estimate of BOS's contribution to elementary school education is lower, at 69 percent of total elementary school education revenues, and the contribution of district and provincial government is higher, at 15 and 11 percent, respectively. This difference suggests that district and provincial BOS and aid are relatively concentrated in some areas.

Figure 4.1
Percentage of Total School Revenues, by Source and Region, 2010

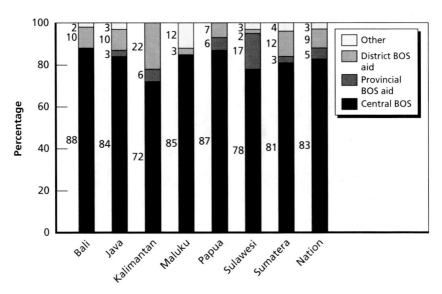

SOURCE: World Bank SBM National Survey (2010), administrative data reported by schools.
NOTE: N = 399 schools.
RAND *MG1229-4.1*

Per-Student Revenue Differed Greatly Across Regions and Schools

Elementary schools in Indonesia received an average of U.S. $75 per student.[3] However, this amount differed greatly across regions (Figure 4.2) and within regions between urban and rural areas. Maluku and Papua schools received nearly half the resources per student than Kalimantan and Java schools, which received nearly U.S. $80 per student. Rural schools had about half the revenues per student that urban schools had: U.S. $71 and $157, respectively.

---

[3] To translate rupiahs into dollars, we used the average exchange rate over the first six months of 2010, the time during which we collected these data. This average exchange rate was 9,190.82.

Figure 4.2
Average School Discretionary Budget per Student, by Region, 2010

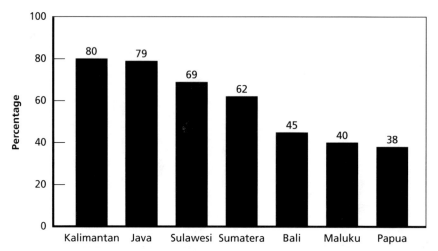

SOURCE: World Bank SBM National Survey (2010), administrative data reported by schools.
NOTE: N = 399 schools.
RAND *MG1229-4.2*

However, the largest variations were across schools. At one extreme, about 9 percent of schools received an average of U.S. $31, which is lower than the U.S. $43 per student presumably allocated to each school nationwide by the central government's BOS program,[4] whereas at the other extreme, 11 percent of schools received an average of U.S. $235 per students, a more than 1 to 7 differential (Figure 4.3).

---

[4]   About 17 percent of schools reported having received less than the Rp 397,000 to 400,000 per student that they should have received under the BOS program. Some, but not all, of the discrepancy may be attributable to differences in number of students between the beginning of the 2009–2010 school year when the BOS funds were allocated and the time of the survey in the spring of 2010. Our data did not permit us to identify other factors that might contribute to these schools having received lower-than-expected BOS revenues per student.

Figure 4.3
Percentage of Schools, by Discretionary Budget per Student, 2010

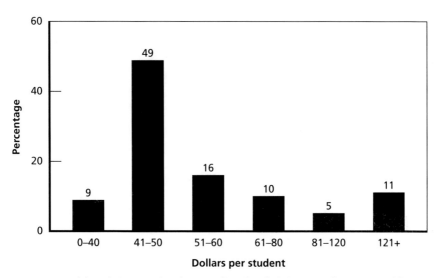

SOURCE: World Bank SBM National Survey (2010), administrative data reported by schools.
NOTE: N = 399 schools.
RAND *MG1229-4.3*

School Stakeholders' Understanding of SBM

Stakeholders' understanding of their roles, authority, and responsibilities under SBM is a prerequisite to its eventual effective implementation by schools.

In the case study schools, principals and teachers reported having a general understanding of school-based management. Typically, they said that it involved exercising the autonomy of the school to manage its own affairs or to involve such stakeholders as the SC, parents, and the community in making school decisions. In the words of selected principals:

> It offers authority for schools, school autonomy; each program can be programmed by involving the school.

It involves school cooperation with other stakeholders outside school, like school committee and parents.

It is school autonomy so school regulates or provides all needs by themselves.

And similarly, from various school teachers:

School is given authority to manage all programs as optimally as possible in order to improve the vision and mission of both the students and the school.

Principal, teacher and school committee are given the authority to govern the school in a better way in order to improve educational quality.

SBM is management in the hands of the school along with stakeholders, that's all I know.

Most principals and teachers also knew that the ultimate purpose of SBM is to improve student learning. Some teachers added that it also was meant to promote cooperation among stakeholders, the school, and parents and the involvement of the community.

However, their understanding seemed to remain at this very general level. When asked why they did not set up a team to implement SBM, they generally responded that they did not do so because they really did not have enough understanding of what SBM consists of:[5]

I don't know the essence of SBM, so can't set up a team.

I only know SBM theory.

---

[5] In responses to the survey, 27 of the 40 sampled schools said that they had an SBM team; however, when asked during the case studies to identify staff who were members of this team, all said that they actually did not have a team. Obviously, there appears to have been a strong incentive for principals to suggest that they were implementing SBM even though they were not sure what it consists of.

That thing needs to be taught first.

Because I don't understand what SBM is until now . . . don't know what the roles of the SC, parents and society are.

Because [we received] no socialization on how SBM should be done.

Alternatively they said they were too busy to implement SBM:

I do not have time to invite parents for meetings. . . . I have to go to meetings with district, KKG [teacher working groups], and KKS [principal conferences] meetings.

I am busy with other problems.

I have not received order from the government.

As for SC members, they did not know what SBM was, if they had even heard about it. In only a few instances did focus group SC members say that they knew they had a role in managing their school's BOS. Similarly, a majority of them also did not know what the goal of SBM was.

The lack of depth in the school principals' knowledge of SBM is not surprising. Only about one-third of principals reported that they had learned about SBM in workshops or socialization sessions provided by their district. Most others learned about SBM from various other sources, including principal working group meetings and newspapers; some could not remember where they heard of it.

As for focus group teachers, none reported receiving socialization on SBM from their district. They learned about SBM from a wide variety of sources including KKG meetings, from SurveyMeter[6] when the school was surveyed in the previous year, from their principal, or from television.

---

[6]   SurveyMeter is the Indonesian company that fielded the study's surveys and conducted the case study focus groups and interviews of principals.

Principal Preparedness, Leadership, and Knowledge

To support SBM, the principal has to be an expert in playing the broader managerial roles that accompany school self-management, promoting collaboration in decisionmaking, engaging and facilitating the work of committees and teachers, and managing operational and instructional matters. Furthermore, the school leader has to have knowledge about the roles and responsibilities of the various committees, including their SC and BOS teams, which are central to SBM in the Indonesian model. The extent to which principals have these competencies will affect how well SBM is implemented.

Principals Were Moderately Prepared to Manage Their Schools

The majority of principals (over 93 percent) reported that they were *at least* adequately prepared to lead and manage various aspects of their schools. However, less than half of the principals indicated that they were "well prepared" in areas central to SBM implementation, including, "providing leadership and vision for school staff," "planning for the school academic improvement in the medium term," "planning and managing the school budget finances," and "making decisions on the school curriculum." By contrast, over 50 percent of principals viewed themselves as being "well prepared" in "supervising and evaluating their teachers" and "engaging and seeking input from teachers and the community" (Figure 4.4). Principals of urban schools were more likely than principals of rural schools to say that they were "well prepared."

Consistent with principal self-reports, supervisors rated the majority of principals as having *at least* adequate preparation to take various school roles. However, their reported percentage of well-prepared principals was substantially lower.

The Functions of the School Committee Were Not Fully Understood by Principals

Principals were not familiar with *all* the roles for which the SC is responsible. About three-quarters of the principals erroneously identified *two or more* functions as the responsibility of the SC (Figure 4.5).

Figure 4.4
Percentage of Principals Prepared to Do Selected Tasks, by Level of Preparation and Type of Task, 2010

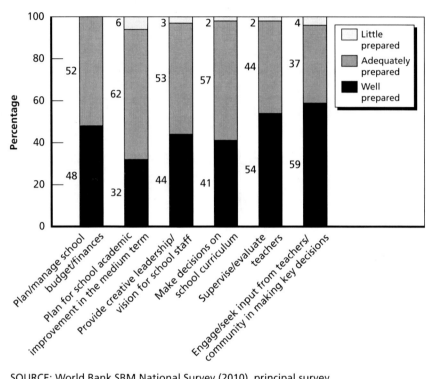

SOURCE: World Bank SBM National Survey (2010), principal survey.
NOTE: N = 400 principals.
RAND MG1229-4.4

For instance, a majority of principals erroneously thought that the SC should approve school policies and make final decisions about how the school operates. There was no difference between urban and rural school principals.

Principals Received BOS Information, but Some Still Lacked Knowledge of Its Purpose

Eighty-three percent of the principals reported receiving a copy of, or having access to, the BOS manual that provides information and

Figure 4.5
Percentage of Principals, by Number of Errors in Identifying SC Responsibilities, 2010

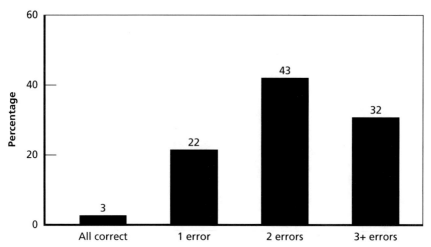

SOURCE: World Bank SBM National Survey (2010), principal survey.
NOTES: N = 394 principals. Respondents were asked which of the following functions are the responsibilities of the SC: A. to provide input on school policies and academic programs but leave final decisions to school leaders (yes); B. to approve policies and make final decisions about how the school operates (no); C. to help raise money donations for the school (yes); D. to provide input in the allocation of BOS funds (yes); E. to verify and approve the school budget (no); F. to conduct regular or intermittent meetings with school parents and the community (yes).
RAND MG1229-4.5

guidance about the BOS program, including information on how to use BOS funds. A majority of school principals reported that they understood the main purposes of BOS. However, about 40 percent misunderstood *two or more* BOS responsibilities (Figure 4.6). About half of the principals reported that one purpose of BOS is to free all families from paying for education. Another misconception that principals had about BOS was that its funds could be used to pay teacher salary increases (25 percent).[7]

---

[7]   BOS funds can be used to make "payments of monthly honoraria for temporary teachers and teaching staff" but cannot be used to pay teacher salary increases.

Figure 4.6
Percentage of Principals, by Number of Errors in Identifying BOS Goals, 2010

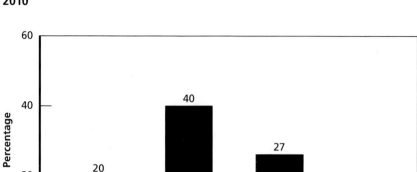

SOURCE: World Bank SBM National Survey (2010), principal survey.
NOTES: N = 364 principals. Respondents were asked which of the following are the purposes of BOS: A. free poor families from paying for education of their children (yes); B. free all families from paying for education (no); C. pay teacher salary increases (no); D. emphasize transparency on school finances and expenditures (yes); E. provide funds to upgrade school facilities (no); F. provide schools with more autonomy (yes).
RAND *MG1229-4.6*

Teacher Preparedness and Knowledge

PNS teachers had higher educational levels but had similar years of teaching experience as non-PNS teachers. Three-quarters of PNS teachers reported having a Diploma IV level Bachelor in Education in either science or other, whereas less than one-third (30 percent) of non-PNS teachers had attained this level of education. Half of non-PNS teachers had reached only the Diploma I/II level, and about 18 percent reported having only elementary, junior, or high school experience. Both PNS and non-PNS teachers reported having an average of 16 years of teaching experience (for a comparison of the characteristics of PNS and non-PNS teachers, see Appendix C).

Teachers Were Also Moderately Prepared

As with principals, nearly all teachers reported that they were at least adequately prepared to provide high-quality education, with about half of them (across five areas of classroom instructional practices) saying that they were "well prepared." Teachers reported that they were least prepared to use a variety of instructional methods in the classroom and plan effective lessons (Figure 4.7).

Over 90 percent of district heads and supervisors, principals, and SC chairs and members also rated teachers as "adequately to well prepared" to provide high-quality education, although the share of teachers rated "well prepared" was lower than the share of teachers who rated themselves well prepared. Teachers' self-assessment of their preparation was the same for PNS and non-PNS teachers. Teachers in

Figure 4.7
Percentage of Teachers Prepared to Do Selected Tasks, by Level of Preparation and Type of Task, 2010

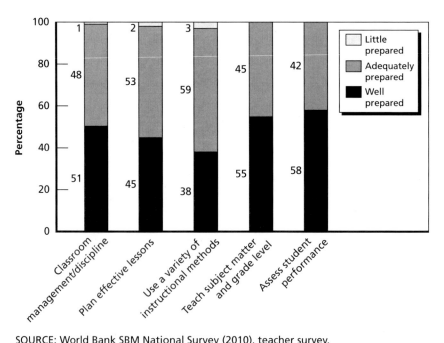

SOURCE: World Bank SBM National Survey (2010), teacher survey.
NOTE: N = 2,353 teachers.
RAND *MG1229-4.7*

urban and rural schools reported being equally prepared, unlike principals as noted above.

Teachers Lacked Knowledge of the Purposes of BOS

Forty-one percent of the teachers understood either all or almost all of the purposes of BOS. A majority (59 percent) had *at least two* misconceptions about the goals of BOS. For example, about two-thirds of the teachers thought erroneously that a main purpose of the BOS funds is to free all families from paying for education. Another quarter thought BOS funds could be used for facility upgrades,[8] whereas a similar proportion (20 percent) either thought the funds could be used for teacher salary increases or were unaware that BOS was expected to provide schools with more autonomy.

School Committee Preparedness and Knowledge

School committees are central to Indonesia's SBM model. These committees are meant to be the vehicles of parental and community participation in school governance and management and are expected to advise school leadership on day-to-day school operations. Their role covers a broad range of areas, from providing input for school planning and program development to ensuring financial transparency. SC members have to have knowledge of their functions and general school operational knowledge to participate successfully in school governance.

School Committee Members Need More Preparation to Do Their Jobs

SC chairs and members reported that they were "somewhat" competent in providing input about school policies, budget, and programs (average scores of 3.8 and 3.9 on a scale from 1 to 6). District heads and supervisors provided similar assessments of school committees' knowledge and skills (average score of 3.7). Principals and teachers, however, had more positive views of SC members' skills, although they still fell

---

[8] BOS funds can be used only for facility maintenance and small repairs, such as painting and repairing a leaky roof.

short of reaching the competent level (average score of 4.2 and 4.4) (Table 4.1).

SC Members Did Not Clearly Understand Their Roles

A large percentage of SC chairs (92 percent) and members (88 percent) had at least two misconceptions about the SC's roles (Figure 4.8). As with principals, the most common error was about SC's approving school policies and making final decisions. A contributing reason for this lack of understanding of the SC role by school stakeholders is that, unlike for BOS, detailed operational guidelines for SC members have yet to be developed by the Ministry of National Education. The SC chairs in urban schools were more likely to be correct about the SC roles than were SC chairs in rural schools.

Although more detailed directives were available to help implement BOS at the school level, about two-thirds of school chairs (61 percent) reported that they did not receive or have access to the BOS

Table 4.1
SC Members' Competency, by Type of Stakeholder Assessment, 2010

Type of Stakeholder	Mean
Principal	4.2
Teacher	4.4
SC chair	3.8
SC member	3.9
District head	3.7
Subdistrict head	4.3
District supervisor head	3.7

SOURCE: World Bank SBM National Survey (2010), all surveys.

NOTES: N = 394 principals, 2,299 teachers, 392 SC chairs, 388 SC members, 54 district heads, 47 subdistrict heads, and 54 district supervisor heads. The competency range is from 1 (not competent) to 6 (very competent).

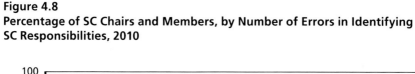

Figure 4.8
Percentage of SC Chairs and Members, by Number of Errors in Identifying SC Responsibilities, 2010

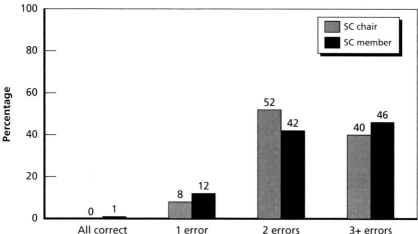

SOURCE: World Bank SBM National Survey (2010), SC chair and SC member surveys.
NOTE: N = 393 SC chairs and 388 SC members. Resondents were asked which of the following functions are the responsibilities of the SC: A. to provide input on school policies and academic programs but leave final decisions to school leaders (yes); B. to approve policies and make final decisions about how the school operates (no); C. to help raise money donations for the school (yes); D. to provide input in the allocation of BOS funds (yes); E. to verify and approve the school budget (no); F. to conduct regular or intermittent meetings with school parents and the community (yes).
RAND *MG1229-4.8*

manual. This unavailability of BOS information may be one reason why committee chairs and members were not fully aware of its purposes. More than half of SC chairs and two-thirds of SC members misunderstood *two or more* of BOS main purposes.

School Committees Received Insufficient Information About Their Schools

SC members were less likely than committee chairs to receive information about their schools. Sixty percent of SC members did not receive information from their school's principal about academic programs, and over 40 percent reported not receiving information about teacher performance, school expenditures, and extracurricular activities (Figure 4.9). Similarly, a substantial proportion of chairs also reported not receiving information on the school's academic programs (53 percent) and the performance of teachers at their school (42 percent). When they had received information, the majority of chairs and members rated it as sufficient.

Challenges to SBM Implementation

A key challenge to effective implementation of SBM in Indonesia, as noted above, is that a plurality of principals, teachers, and SC mem-

Figure 4.9
Percentage of SC Members Receiving Information from Principal, by Type and Level of Adequacy of Information, 2010

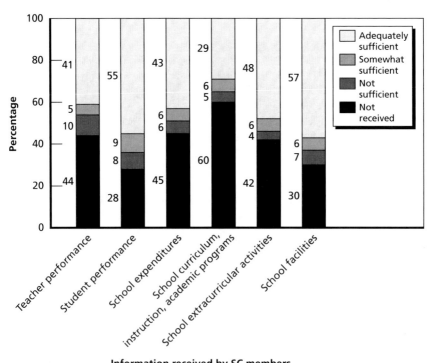

Information received by SC members

SOURCE: World Bank SBM National Survey (2010), SC member survey.
NOTE: N = 388 SC members.
RAND MG1229-4.9

bers did not understand its goals, purposes, and responsibilities. In the words of various principals who were interviewed in the case studies:

> It is difficult because we do not understand 100 percent yet about SBM. We only know that SBM is all about our relationship with society, that's all. The details should be socialized to the school.

> We only know about the meaning of it [SBM], just in the surface, so we will need the information on how the implementation of SBM should be.

> I don't really understand about SBM, so I need socialization about it and get more frequent visits from the district.

SC focus group participants similarly said that the main challenge to their effective involvement in school affairs was their lack of understanding of their role and responsibilities under SBM:

> So far, we are only elected without knowing our job.

> It is the biggest difficulty for SC, because we know nothing of the steps and the purpose for the committee or how to handle school duties.

> The SC main work is to monitor the school's physical environment. The curriculum is no concern.

> Honestly, all of SC's involvement is the formality to complete the administration.

In addition, a few principals seemed somewhat confused about the distribution of responsibilities between districts and schools under SBM:

> For example, if there is a damaged building, whose responsibility is it to repair it? The principal may submit a proposal to the education office to make repairs, but if the building collapses in the interim, who is to blame, the principal or the district?

Beyond their inadequate understanding of what is expected of them under SBM, a majority of surveyed principals and district staff indicated that a complementary challenge was "insufficient school staff knowledge and expertise to make policy and program decisions" (Table 4.2). Without school staff expertise to align their academic and other programs with local needs and priorities, the promise of SBM cannot be effectively fulfilled.

"Insufficient parent participation in school affairs" and "insufficient funding" were also hindrances frequently reported by both district staff and principals. By contrast, only a small proportion of both types of stakeholders felt that "insufficient district support" or "insufficient principal autonomy" were hindrances to effective implementation of SBM.

A critical challenge to improving student achievement mentioned by many teachers interviewed in the case study was insufficient infor-

Table 4.2
Percentage of Stakeholders Who Reported Moderate to Great Hindrances, by Type of Hindrance and Type of Stakeholder, 2009–2010

Type of Hindrance	District Head	Subdistrict Head	District Supervisor Head	Principal
Insufficient staff knowledge and expertise to make policy and program decisions	57	72	38	38
Insufficient principal training about SBM	57	71	42	49
Insufficient time to hold meetings with stakeholders	31	40	54	39
Insufficient district support	17	18	21	24
Insufficient principal authority to make decisions	27	27	25	20
Insufficient parent participation in school affairs	67	49	46	45
Insufficient funding	68	58	61	57

SOURCE: World Bank SBM National Survey (2010), district head, subdistrict head, district supervisor head, and principal surveys.

NOTE: N = 54 district heads, 47 subdistrict heads, 54 district supervisor heads, and 400 principals.

mation on what to do to improve learning. This became apparent when we asked schools about their key priorities. Nearly all principals, teachers, and SC members indicated that it was "to improve quality of education," which in the majority of case study schools meant seeking to maximize the number of sixth-graders passing the National Exam, in part because it is a prerequisite for students who wish to continue their education in public junior high school:

> We want all students to pass 6th grade so they are accepted in the next level, otherwise, they have to go to private school and that is hard financially on parents. (Teacher)

> The priority is the children could graduate and get accepted in public junior high school. (Principal)

Not only was the top priority the same across most schools, the actions taken to prepare students to pass the National Exam were also the same. Schools provided out-of-regular-hours remedial tutoring or extra lessons to sixth-graders, although sometimes also to students in earlier grades. Parents were also encouraged, with the help of SC members, to support their children's education by allowing them to attend these extra lessons and by promoting a home environment supportive of studying, such as restricting television viewing. This uniformity of interventions across most case study schools suggests a lack of knowledge of alternatives in addressing student performance issues. It also suggests that schools have yet to take advantage of the flexibility provided to them by SBM or that districts continue to maintain close control over school practices.

Summary

The capacity of elementary schools to implement SBM is relatively low and varied across schools. Most importantly, the amount of resources available varied broadly across provinces and schools. Although the average per-student school revenue was U.S. $75, at one extreme, some schools received less than half of this amount, and at the other extreme, some received more than three times this amount. This is due in part to some province and district governments providing operating revenues in addition to the central government's BOS funds to some of their schools, most particularly urban schools. Overall, in 2009–2010, BOS revenues accounted for 83 percent of the average school revenues, whereas district revenues accounted for 9 percent and province revenues accounted for 5 percent. Donations from parents were minimal.

Understanding of the concept and purposes of SBM differed between schools and across type of stakeholders. Principals and teachers indicated that they generally understood the autonomy it provided schools to make managerial and programmatic decisions with input from other stakeholders, but they did not quite know what to make of it operationally. Only a minority of principals indicated that they were well prepared to deal with areas central to SBM, such as "providing creative leadership and vision for school staff," "planning for the school's academic improvement in the medium term," "planning and managing the school budget and finances," and "making decisions on the school curriculum." As for SC members and parents, their participation in SBM was hampered by their lack of knowledge about SBM. They were nearly unanimous in indicating that they did not know what SBM was, if they even had heard of it.

Knowledge about the roles the SC should play in SBM and the purposes of the BOS programs was also uneven across school stakeholders. About three-quarters of principals had misconceptions about two or more out of six different functions attributed to the SC, and about 40 percent of principals and teachers had misconceptions about two or more out of seven different ways that central BOS funds could be used, including the misconception that it freed all families from paying a fee for education. In turn, a majority of SC chairs and members indicated that they were unclear about the full set of responsibilities and authority given to school committees, including their advisory role. In addition, about 60 percent of school committees reported that they did not get adequate information about their school's policies and programs to support their activities.

Several hindrances were identified by a majority of principals and district staff, the most notable of which were insufficient training about

SBM and insufficient staff knowledge and expertise to make operational and programmatic decisions. Insufficient funding was also mentioned frequently by district staff and principals, whereas insufficient time to hold meetings with stakeholders was mentioned less frequently.

School principals and teachers reported that they were otherwise adequately to well prepared to manage their schools or classrooms, respectively. District staff, including supervisors, generally agreed with this self-assessment, although they were somewhat less positive about the adequacy of principals' and teachers' preparation. These positive self-views about school staff preparation may be an obstacle to improving schools and student performance, as too few stakeholders at the district and school levels see a major need for improvement.

District Support of SBM Implementation

Research suggests that how districts support schools in their implementation of SBM, by providing information, guidelines, training, and on-site technical assistance and mentoring, is likely to affect how SBM is actually implemented as intended (Fullan, 2001; Caldwell and Wood, 1988; USAID, 2011). In this chapter, we explore how the Indonesian education districts provided support for SBM implementation. This support may have come in various forms. It may include the provision of training or socialization, sharing of information, or guidance to school leaders and other school stakeholders, including SC members, for the purpose of expanding their knowledge and skills on how to set school visions, monitor budgets, develop work plans, organize committee meetings, and monitor performance. District support may also target teachers, who are central to SBM, by developing their knowledge in the areas of teaching, learning, and curriculum.

District Involvement and Reach

The majority of district leaders reported that their districts were "very involved" in the provision of training addressed by the BOS program (90 percent). About three-quarters of the districts were "very involved" in providing schools with training on SBM responsibilities and improving school capacity to implement SBM. However, districts tended to be less involved in providing training on SC policies (Figure 5.1).

A majority of districts also reported helping schools formulate their curriculum and annual plans (60 percent). A smaller percentage

Figure 5.1
Percentage of Districts Providing SBM-Related Training, by Type of Training and Extent of Involvement, 2010

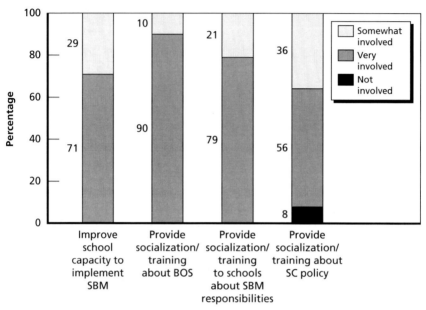

SOURCE: World Bank SBM National Survey (2010), district head survey.
NOTE: N = 54 district heads.
RAND MG1229-5.1

reported helping schools formulate their instructional and student test materials (Figure 5.2).

Still, a sizable share of districts, from 27 to 62 percent depending on the SBM-related activity, reported providing no assistance to schools.

Principal Training

Most Subdistricts Provided Principals with a Variety of SBM-Related Training in 2009–2010

About three-quarters of subdistricts reported providing training on the development of schools' annual plans (78 percent), planning and man-

Figure 5.2
Percentage of Districts Providing Assistance, by Type of Assistance, 2010

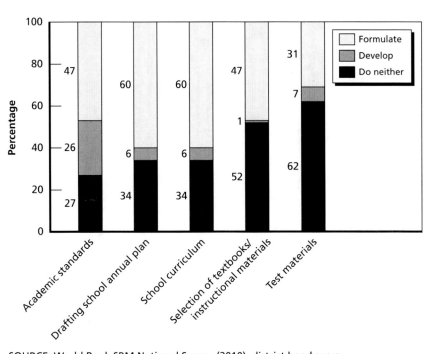

SOURCE: World Bank SBM National Survey (2010), district head survey.
NOTE: N = 54 district heads.
RAND MG1229-5.2

agement of school budget (60 percent), working with school committees (68 percent), and promotion of teacher development (66 percent).
About two-thirds of subdistricts provided principals with training on
the implementation of BOS (65 percent) (Figure 5.3).

The Majority of Principals Attended at Least One Day of Training

Eighty-three percent of principals reported receiving some form of
training during the 2009–2010 school year, although the training
received was short in duration. About 31 percent of principals received
one to two days of training from all sources including the Ministry of
National Education, provincial government, district, subdistrict, and

Figure 5.3
Percentage of Subdistricts Providing SBM-Related Training to Principals, by Type of Training, 2010

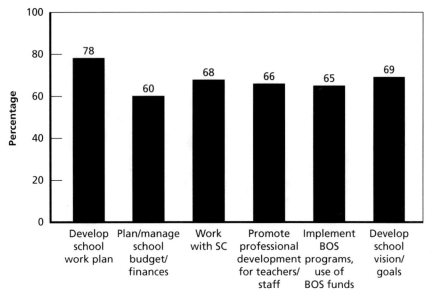

SOURCE: World Bank SBM National Survey (2010), subdistrict head survey.
NOTE: N = 47 subdistrict heads.
RAND *MG1229-5.3*

private foundations.[1] A slightly larger proportion of principals received between three and eight training days, and the remaining principals reported attending more than eight days of training (Figure 5.4). Principals in urban schools were more likely than principals in rural schools to have received no training.

However, a Majority of Principals Were Not Trained or Sufficiently Trained in Key SBM-Related Activities

Not all principals received training in important SBM-related areas. About half of principals did not receive training during the 2009–2010

---

[1]   Few principals and teachers surveyed (10 and 22 percent, respectively) received any training from private foundations or donors, and when they did, the training was limited to one or two days.

Figure 5.4
Percentage of Principals Receiving Training, by Number of Training Days,
2009–2010

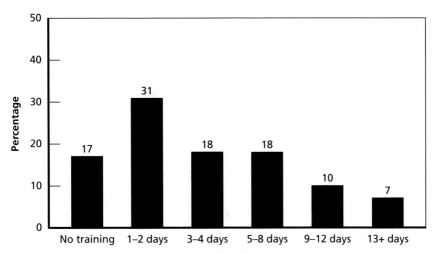

SOURCE: World Bank SBM National Survey (2010), principal survey.
NOTES: N = 400 principals. Percentages may not sum to 100 percent because of
rounding.
RAND *MG1229-5.4*

school year on how to develop a school mission and vision, annual plan, curriculum, and school budget and how to supervise and evaluate teachers and work with school committees (Figure 5.5). Training addressing parental involvement and community members in supporting schools was minimal, with 71 percent of principals reporting receiving no such training.

Principals who received training often rated it as inadequate. For training related to the development of a school vision, an annual plan, or a school's curriculum, approximately half of the principals receiving training reported that the training was either "not sufficient" or "somewhat sufficient" in meeting their needs. For other types of training, a larger percentage of principals indicated that the training they received was enough to meet their needs. That was particularly true for BOS (54 percent) and school budget planning (40 percent). However, in the

Figure 5.5
Percentage of Principals Receiving Training, by Type and Adequacy of Training, 2009–2010

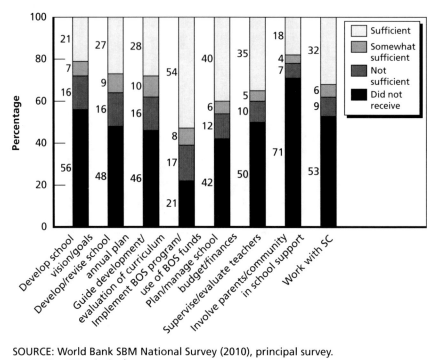

SOURCE: World Bank SBM National Survey (2010), principal survey.
NOTE: N = 400 principals.
RAND *MG1229-5.5*

words of principals who were interviewed in the case study, the training was minimal:

> The socialization was of bookkeeping process and how to pay the tax. That's all.

> I suggested that it is better if such [BOS] training gave real examples taken from school that already run BOS funds well so that we can understand it. The training was only theories and orally, so I did not get it. Thus, I need more consultation with other teachers in other schools.

Principals Agreed That Districts Were Supportive of Their Schools

Still, a majority of principals agreed that their districts provided them with useful feedback on their performance. They also mostly agreed that districts provided their teachers with high-quality professional development and sufficient instructional support, although teachers were less likely to concur (see the "Teacher Training" section, below). A substantial proportion of principals also agreed that their districts understood the particular needs of their school (83 percent).

However, principals did not feel supported by their districts in one aspect. About 60 percent of them indicated that their districts produced policy directives and official guidelines that changed frequently. Such changes have the potential to signal to school stakeholders inconsistent messages regarding SBM purposes, roles, and responsibilities (Figure 5.6).

Figure 5.6
Percentage of Principals Agreeing That Districts Were Supportive of Their Schools, by Type of Support, 2010

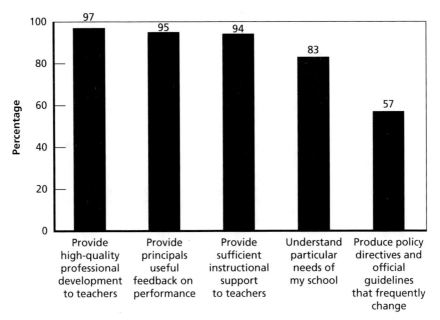

SOURCE: World Bank SBM National Survey (2010), principal survey.
NOTE: N = 400 principals.
RAND MG1229-5.6

Teacher Training

Most Subdistricts Provided a Variety of SBM-Related Training for Teachers

Subdistricts were as likely to provide training in various areas to teachers as to principals. About two-thirds of subdistricts reported providing training to teachers, the same proportion as for principals. Training provided tended to emphasize areas relevant to teachers' everyday activities and may provide a basis for directly improving student learning, such as instructional methods (65 percent) and lesson planning and classroom management (64 percent). About 60 percent of subdistricts also reported providing training to teachers that was SBM-specific, including how to prepare the school's work plan and assess the school's needs and set goals (Figure 5.7).

Figure 5.7
Percentage of Subdistricts Providing SBM-Related Training to Teachers, by Type of Training, 2010

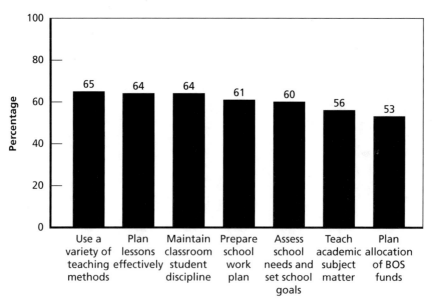

SOURCE: World Bank SBM National Survey (2010), subdistrict head survey.
NOTE: N = 47 subdistrict heads.
RAND *MG1229-5.7*

However, Training Did Not Reach Half of Teachers

About half of teachers (48 percent) reported not receiving any training or staff development during school year 2009–2010 from any governmental, local, or private sources (Figure 5.8). In the words of one representative teacher who participated in case study focus groups:

> There is no training. It is very difficult to conduct training [in the school], because all of the members are hard to gather at one time. There should be competence training, how to supervise. Hopefully UPTD [district education office] and education department can facilitate it.

At the same time, case study principals and teachers said that there were many training or workshop opportunities on specific topics ranging from the arts to the sciences, a thematic approach to the curriculum, teaching methods, reading, leadership, syllabus development, and SBM. However, only one or two teachers at a time and from any

Figure 5.8
Percentage of Teachers Receiving Training, by Number of Training Days, 2010

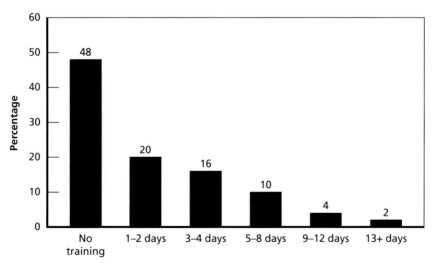

SOURCE: World Bank SBM National Survey (2010), teacher survey.
NOTE: N = 2,353 teachers.
RAND *MG1229-5.8*

one school were typically sent to take advantage of available training opportunities, with the expectation that the participants would then share their gained knowledge with their colleagues in a kind of "train the trainers" approach.

Also, most of the workshops were of short duration, and some of our respondents who participated in them said that they had already forgotten what they had learned. The duration of training for most teachers who received any training was from one to four days. A small percentage of teachers (16 percent) received one week or more of staff development (Figure 5.8). There was no difference in training received by teachers at urban and rural schools.

As with Principals, a Majority of Teachers Were Not Trained or Sufficiently Trained in Key SBM-Related Activities

Over three-quarters of teachers indicated that they had received no training that addressed classroom management, planning the allocation of BOS funds, assessing school needs and setting school goals, or preparing the school's work plan. About two-thirds reported not receiving training on how to teach their subject matter or how to assess their students, and over half of the teachers were not provided with training on lesson planning or how to use a variety of instructional methods. In these areas, another 10 percent or so reported that they were "not sufficiently" or "somewhat sufficiently" trained (Figure 5.9).

Teachers Were Provided with Valuable Information Through Their KKG Participation

The majority of teachers (87 percent) participated in teacher working group (KKG) meetings. Teachers tended to find the information they received in these meetings to be moderately to very useful. More than half of teachers found the information provided at KKG meetings to be very useful in informing them of how to develop their syllabi and lesson plans, develop student tests, and enhance their knowledge of the curriculum and their subject matter (Figure 5.10):

> In KKG, we bring our issues from school in order to be solved together, so there is a kind of guidance or materials. Hence, con-

Figure 5.9
Percentage of Teachers Receiving Training, by Type and Adequacy of Training, 2010

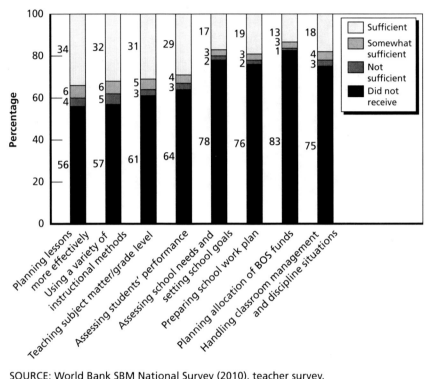

SOURCE: World Bank SBM National Survey (2010), teacher survey.
NOTE: N = 2,353 teachers.
RAND MG1229-5.9

cerns that cannot be solved by an individual school, such as in mathematics, can be addressed and solved in the KKG.

[KKG] improves education quality in each school, to complete administration, improve the drafting of test questions. After teachers follow KKG, they make improvements on the way they design test during learning process.

Figure 5.10
Percentage of Teachers Participating in KKG Meetings, by Topic Discussed and Usefulness of Information Received, 2010

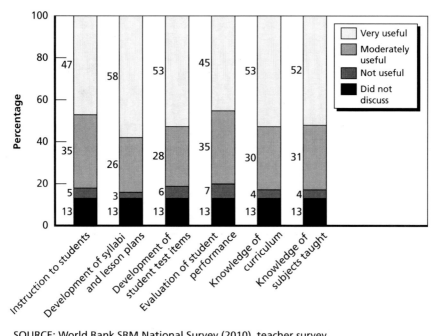

SOURCE: World Bank SBM National Survey (2010), teacher survey.
NOTE: N = 2,353 teachers.
RAND MG1229-5.10

School Committee Training

SC Members Received Little Training on their BOS and SC Responsibilities

About two-thirds of subdistricts reported providing training on BOS, and about two-thirds of subdistricts reported providing training on SC members' roles and responsibilities.

However, during school years 2008–2009 and 2009–2010, about three-fourths of the surveyed SC members reported that they did not receive training on BOS. A substantial, although smaller, percentage of SC chairs (42 percent) also reported not receiving BOS training. And when provided, the duration of training was minimal, typically consisting of one day or less for most SC members (Figure 5.11).

Figure 5.11
Percentage of SC Chairs and Members, by Whether They Received BOS Training and the Hours of Training Received, 2008–2010

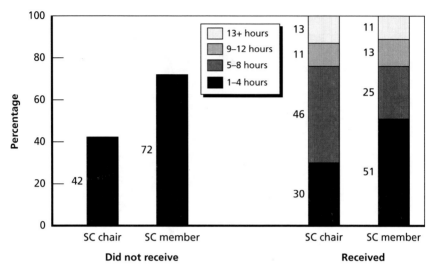

SOURCE: World Bank SBM National Survey (2010), SC chair and SC member surveys.
NOTE: N = 391 SC chairs and 379 SC members.
RAND MG1229-5.11

SC chairs and members, similarly, received no or minimal training on their roles and responsibilities. About two-thirds of surveyed SC members and one-third of SC chairs reported receiving no training in the previous two years. When training was received, it was minimal in duration. Three-quarters of the members and about half of the chairs received eight or fewer hours of training. SC members in rural schools were somewhat less likely to report having received training than were SC members in urban schools.

Nevertheless, the majority of those who attended training sessions in the previous two years (2008–2009 and 2009–2010) indicated that the information they received on their roles and responsibilities and on the type of members who should serve had been sufficient and had met their needs. Chairs and members reported more dissatisfaction with the information they received on the roles and responsibilities of the SC than with other types of information (Figure 5.12).

Figure 5.12
Percentage of SC Members Who Received SC Training, by Type and Adequacy of SC Training, 2008–2010

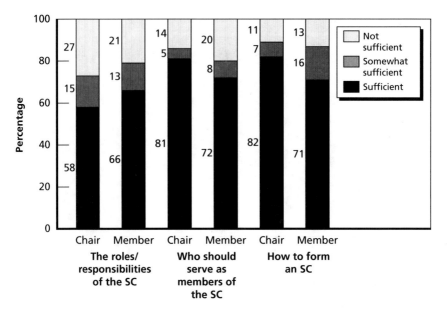

SOURCE: World Bank SBM National Survey (2010), SC chair and SC member survey.
NOTE: N = 134–228 SC chairs and 88–98 SC members.
RAND *MG1229-5.12*

Assistance Desired to Make Schools Better

In the case study, we asked principals and focus group participants several questions about the assistance they needed to improve SBM and the three most important things that would make their school better. Overall, respondents indicated that the assistance they would like to receive fell into two major categories:

- improvements to school's physical facilities
- support for teachers in the classroom.

Improvement of School Facilities

The need to upgrade school facilities was expressed by nearly every school. The kind of materials and improvements needed ranged from such small items as tables and chairs for students to larger items including bookshelves, a fence or gate to improve school security, classrooms to alleviate overcrowded classrooms, or a room to house a library, laboratory, health unit, or principal's office.

Support for Teachers in the Classrooms

Teachers and principals in about half of the case study schools said that they would like to receive more training or refresher courses in various areas including teaching methods, academic content, a thematic approach to teaching the curriculum, and in general how to be more effective teachers. They also asked for more in-depth training on the goals, purposes, and responsibilities of SBM. Some teachers also felt that the training needed should be better distributed across teachers:

> If we have training it must be spread more evenly, not to be monopolized by one group, because some of us have never attended training while others have had it often.

Teachers in most case study schools also wanted access to more teaching tools or props. The teaching aids they needed ranged from such simple props as maps, globes, or scales to visual aids (LCD and projectors) or science and math kits. Laptops were also often mentioned by teachers, as was the need for more books to complement the textbooks used in lessons:

> Teacher props are few and need to be added. Computers we want to add like in the cities. There is information and communications technology. We don't have it here.

Other Suggested Actions or Forms of Assistance

A frequent theme in many comments from principals, teachers, and SC members was to encourage better parental supervision and support of children to increase students' attendance and studying discipline. Although mentioned less frequently than student attendance, better teacher attendance and timeliness was said to be particularly important to serve as a model for students.

More frequent monitoring and mentoring by district staff was another action that was thought would be particularly helpful by both principals and teachers. As noted above, some schools and teachers reported that they were rarely visited by district staff and that this staff did not know the conditions of their schools, implying that if they did they would provide more assistance:

> If we are supervised continuously, we will work more diligently, won't come lax if the supervisor is here.

> More supervision for teachers would increase their spirit, give motivation, and provide information about other changes that teachers should do to improve work performance.

SC members suggested four actions that would improve their effectiveness. The most frequently mentioned, by half of the case study focus groups, was training or guidance on what their roles and duties are and how to carry them out. As noted above, most SC chairs and members indicated that they did not know what their functions were and that no one had defined them, leaving the active involvement of the SC in school affairs pretty much at the school principal's discretion:

> The school committee should be trained about its rights, responsibilities and job description to avoid misconceptions. So far there has been no guidance.

> If government pays attention to SC, then SC will give more attention to schools. As government treats SC only as a symbol, we automatically just take it easy.

A second action suggested by some SC members as well as some principals and teachers was to give them an honorarium to, among other things, cover transportation costs, thereby encouraging more active participation in school affairs. A third action suggested by a few SC chairs was to have the decree for the formation of the SC issued by the district education office instead of the principal. It was thought that this would give the SC more legitimacy as well as independence from the school.

Finally, several respondents indicated that they would like the policy about school fund-raising to be clarified in the direction of allowing schools and their SCs to raise funds from parents. There is still much confusion about whether schools are authorized to raise funds from parents, with many schools under the impression that they are not permitted to do so:

> We would be at risk if we asked contributions from parents.

Summary

Two-thirds to three-quarters of districts and subdistricts reported providing training and other support to implement SBM. They said that they provided principals and teachers with training or socialization on SBM and BOS, but less than half of districts or subdistricts said that they provided socialization about the SC's role in SBM. They helped formulate schools' academic standards, work plans, and curricula and helped schools select textbooks and instructional materials. Principals generally agreed that districts were supportive and understood the needs of their schools.

Although districts and other governmental and nongovernmental entities were offering many training and assistance opportunities (confirmed by focus group teachers and principals), few principals and teachers said that they had benefited from them. A majority of principals and teachers reported either that they had received no training in the past year in key SBM-related activities or that the training received was insufficient. An average of 70 percent of principals and an average of about 80 percent of teachers had not received any training or found the training not sufficient or somewhat sufficient on developing a school's vision and annual plan, making the best use of budget resources, developing the curriculum, and dealing with instructional issues, including planning lessons and teaching their subject matter. When received, most of the training or socialization lasted a day or two and some of the teachers in focus groups who had received some training said that they had already forgotten what they had learned.

Training of SC members about their roles and responsibilities had also been sporadic over the previous two years. About 60 percent of SC chairs and one-third of SC members reported receiving some training. However, the majority said that the training amounted to less than eight hours.

Improvement to school facilities and training were the two types of assistance most frequently desired by school stakeholders to make their school better and increase student learning. The expressed facility needs were broad, ranging from needing chairs and desks for students to adding classrooms to alleviate overcrowding. Desired principal and teacher training ranged from teaching methods to academic content and included a wish for more socialization about the purposes of and responsibilities under SBM. Other actions desired by principals and teachers included encouraging parental supervision and support of their children's school attendance and studying and more frequent monitoring and mentoring of teachers by district staff.

CHAPTER SIX

Intermediate Outcomes

The theory of SBM suggests that providing schools and local stakeholders with more flexibility to allocate their budget and select staff, curriculum, and classroom instruction may lead to a better learning environment for students and staff and instructional innovations and academic programs more suited to local student populations. In turn, the combination of these changes is expected to be reflected in increased student achievement. In this chapter, we discuss selected intermediate outcomes of SBM, including how schools spent their disposable resources, the perceived effects of SBM and BOS on a number of education access and quality outcomes, monetary and in-kind support provided by parents, attendance by both students and teachers, and the satisfaction of parents with their child's school. We also discuss the students' performance in Bahasa and mathematics.

Perceived Effects of SBM

Case study principals, teachers, and SC and BOS team members were asked what changes their school had made as a result of SBM over the past two years. Respondents were about evenly split between those who reported some changes and those who reported that little to no change had taken place:

> Not much success we have achieved with this SBM system. However, we have implemented SBM, and also remind the teachers to implement this SBM well.

> No significant changes because we don't understand SBM, so we don't know whether it has had any influence.

Others pointed out to a number of positive changes as described below.

More Interactions with Parents

One effect reported by some principals and teachers was an improved relationship with parents through an increase in the frequency of encounters between parents and teachers:

> We invite the parents more often, for example, if any student lacks discipline, often skip classes, we invite his parents to give them some direction, either individually or per class. This year, we invited parents frequently for socialization.

> With SBM, the relationship between parents and teachers are better. We cooperate in children's matter, about their education and knowledge.

> Nowadays, teachers and parents have more opportunities to meet to discuss school issues.

> Parents more freely give suggestions on the academic improvement of their children. They have become more open to teachers and we can give feedback.

Changes in Teaching Methods

Teachers mentioned a variety of changes they made in their teaching methods, including shifting from lecturing to engaging students in their own active learning, using groupings of students, better relating content with the practical experience of students, and bringing more variety into their teaching:[1]

> We used to teach in a monotonous way, now it has become more varied.

---

[1]   Rather than as a result of SBM, some of the reported changes in teaching methods may be related to the introduction of PAKEM, a student-centered form of instruction.

> We used to use the speech method, but we're involving students now. Students are active. We just monitor them, give them advice.

> We used to know only lecturing as the method of teaching. But, now we have easier job because we serve as facilitator. Children are asked to explore the lessons by themselves, we only give them motivation and encouragement so that they can understand the material given.

> It is not necessary to follow the curriculum exactly; we can adjust the atmosphere by reducing and also adding.

> With SBM we are free to set the method until we find a better one, from seating arrangement, how to make that kid absorb the lesson easily.

> We used to teach by speech, now we also use learning aids.

Some teachers also said that their motivation had been increased so that they were more active and worked harder:

> We are the owner of how we make it better, so the teachers have a motivation to improve school quality.

Many principals also reported that more textbooks and books were now available to students, referring mostly to books complementing the curriculum:

> It used to be one book for one group of students, but now there is one book for each student.

However, only a few teachers said that they had changed textbooks from the one directed by the district or from the one that they had always used:

> Books published in the '90s have been kept, the books are still relevant.

Similarly, few teachers reported that they had made adjustments to their curriculum, and if they did so it was by means of minor additions. To a large extent, textbooks and curriculum seemed to continue to be viewed by teachers and principals as the prerogative of the government.

Finally, only a small share of case study principals said that there were improvements in student performance, which they rated as being small.

School Facility Improvements

SC members were more likely than principals and teachers to point out improvements to the school facility over the past two years that they had helped bring about. Such improvements included building a fence around the school or installing a gate at the entrance of the school, digging a well for clean water, covering the dirt school yard, fixing a leaking roof, painting the school's or classrooms' walls, building a fountain or a small mosque, fixing the toilets, and decorating the school with flowers.

Another somewhat less frequently reported effect of BOS was providing students with shoes and uniforms:

> It had huge influence, students here used to go barefoot. Now thanks to BOS they wear shoes.

Use of School Discretionary Resources

Schools' BOS and other district and provincial resources can be allocated by schools with relative flexibility, with the exception of teacher salaries, which are paid directly and assigned to schools by the central government (see Chapters One and Three).

Discretionary Resources Were Spent Mostly on Instruction-Related Activities

In 2009–2010, schools spent about 60 percent of their discretionary resources on instructional-support activities, and the balance was spent mainly on facility support. Within each of these aggregated categories, expenditures were distributed over a number of items (Figure 6.1).

On average, school expenditures were highest (about 22 percent) for the salaries of non-PNS teachers hired directly by schools to complement the number of teachers assigned by the central government. To date, about one-third of the teaching force is non-PNS. Student testing and reports, and student activities, are the only other categories of instructional support expenditures exceeding 10 percent of total expenditures at 14 and 11 percent, respectively. To the extent that principals and teachers effectively use the test results to address instructional issues or focus on lagging students, such expenditures may have

Figure 6.1
Percentage of Discretionary Expenditures, by Category, 2010

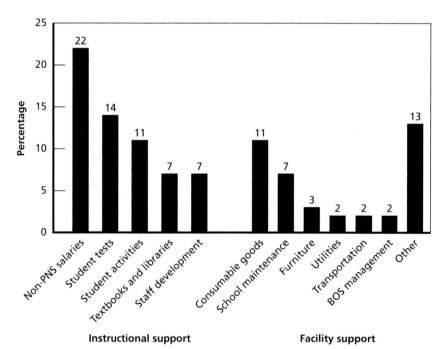

SOURCE: World Bank SBM National Survey (2010), administrative data provided by schools.
NOTE: N = 399 schools. Expenditures are based on the schools' disposable budget.
RAND MG1229-6.1

a positive effect on student achievement. Expenditures on textbooks and library books and on staff development were relatively smaller, at 7 percent of total school expenditures.

Among noninstructional expenditures, about 11 percent of total expenditures was for consumable goods and 7 percent was for school maintenance. No other expenditure amounted to more than 3 percent of total expenditures, including that for utilities and transportation.

Urban schools spent a larger share of their disposable budget (65 percent) on instructional-related activities than did rural schools (59 percent), which is accounted for mostly by larger expenditures to hire and pay non-PNS teachers. Also, expenditures allocated to instruction-related activities differed somewhat across regions. Papua and Maluku spent proportionally less than the other regions on instruction-related activities (Figure 6.2).

Figure 6.2
Percentage of School Discretionary Expenditures for Instruction-Related Activities, by Region, 2010

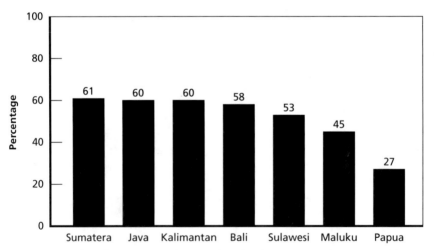

SOURCE: World Bank SBM National Survey (2010), administrative data provided by schools.
NOTE: N = 399 schools.
RAND MG1229-6.2

There Were Large Variations in the Way Schools Spent Their Discretionary Resources

There were large variations in how schools used their disposable resources, with some schools spending nearly nothing on instruction-related expenditures and others spending most of their disposable resources on this aggregated category (Table 6.1). A major source of these variations is expenditures on non-PNS teachers and, to a lesser extent, on student tests and reports. For instance, 11 percent of schools had less than 5 percent non-PNS teachers in their teacher corps whereas at the other extreme, in another 11 percent of schools, more than 50 percent of the teaching staff consisted of non-PNS teachers.

These variations across urban and rural areas, across regions, and across schools suggest that schools may be making choices responding to local conditions, needs, and possibly constraints consistent with SBM expectations. In Chapter Seven, we discuss the factors associated with schools' allocation of expenditures.

Table 6.1
Percentage of Schools and Percentage of Discretionary Budget Spent on Instruction-Related Expenditures, 2010

Percentage Spent on Instruction-Related Items[a]	Percentage of Schools
0–20	5
21–40	8
41–60	26
61–80	56
81–100	4
	100

SOURCE: World Bank SBM National Survey (2010), administrative data provided by schools.

NOTES: N = 399 schools. Percentages do not sum to 100 percent because of rounding.

[a] Items include: non-PNS salaries, student tests, student activities, textbooks and libraries, and staff development.

Effects of BOS Program

BOS Made Schools Better Off

The majority of schools (76 percent) reported that the BOS programs had made them better off financially, and another 17 percent reported no change (Figure 6.3).[2] Schools that were positively affected increased their discretionary revenues by an average of 101 percent, with rural schools increasing their resources more than twice as much as urban schools, 111 percent versus 49 percent. The small share of schools that were negatively affected saw their revenues decline by an average of 18 percent in both rural and urban schools.

The counterpoint to this generally positive effect of the BOS program on school disposable revenues is a reported reduction in fund-

Figure 6.3
Percentage of Schools, by Discretionary Budget Status Before and After the BOS Program, 2010

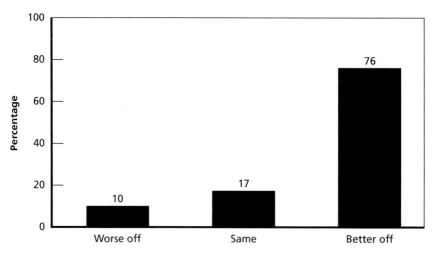

SOURCE: World Bank SBM National Survey (2010), administrative data provided by schools.
NOTE: N = 399 schools.
RAND *MG1229-6.3*

---

[2]   School officers were asked, "Is your school's total operational budget now (school year 2009–2010) bigger than, equal to, or less than before you received BOS funds, and by what percentage?"

raising by nearly two-thirds of schools, with one-quarter reporting no change. These reductions in fund-raising, however, were more than offset by the increase in revenues resulting from the BOS program as noted above.

Effects of BOS on Selected Outcomes Were Reportedly Positive

Asked about the effects of BOS, stakeholders were generally positive. More than 85 percent of school-based respondents across all types agreed that the BOS program had increased student transition to junior high school, the availability of books, and student performance. Fewer respondents, but still about three-quarters, said that the dropout rate had lowered and the authority of the school had increased. A lower proportion, but still a majority of respondents, agreed that fund-raising had decreased and that more poor students were enrolled as a result of the BOS program (Table 6.2).[3]

There were few notable variations across regions. Schools in Maluku and Papua were less likely than schools in the other regions to report that BOS had resulted in less fund-raising. Also, schools in Papua were also less likely to report that books were made more available and that school authority had been increased.

Minimal Parental Contributions

Parents reported making small or no monetary contributions. This is consistent with the reported decrease in fund-raising activities resulting from the BOS program noted above. Nearly 90 percent of parents reported making no monetary contributions, and the remaining mostly made contributions ranging from the equivalent of U.S. $1 to $6.

Parental in-kind contributions were also minimal with one exception. About 20 percent of parents reported they had given time to help in school maintenance. Otherwise, only about 5 percent of parents reported they had contributed time for extracurricular activities or donated construction materials or school equipment. Few reported donating computers, school uniforms, or books.

---

[3]   We did not have actual data to verify these claims.

Table 6.2
Average Percentage of Respondents Agreeing on BOS Effects, by Type of
Effects and Region, 2010

Changes Attributable to BOS	Region						
	Sumatera	Java	Bali	Kalimantan	Sulawesi	Maluku	Papua
Lower dropout rate	76	74	81	74	80	54**	50**
Higher student transition to junior high school	89	90	81**	87	91	86	74**
Less fund-raising in school	63	62	62	58	61	40**	41*
Enrollment of more poor students	69	63	74	60	75	48	68
More available books	91	94	94	87	94	80	50*
Increased school authority	73	76	79	72	75	69	56**
Higher student performance	88	90	92	80	97**	81	81

SOURCE: World Bank SBM National Survey (2010), all surveys.

NOTES: N = 399 schools. Percentages were constructed by taking the average across district heads, school principals, SC heads, SC members, and teachers (equally weighted).

* The mean is significantly different at the 0.01 level.

** The mean is significantly different at the 0.05 level.

Student and Teacher Attendance

Student and teacher daily attendance was reported to be high in most schools. In two-thirds of schools, 98 to 100 percent of students were in school on an average day, and in about two-thirds of schools, less than 5 percent of students arrived late. Teacher attendance was between 98 and 100 percent in 85 percent of schools (Figure 6.4). About three-quarters of teachers reported that they were absent one day or less in the previous month.[4]

High Parental Satisfaction

Parents were generally satisfied with their child's school. Two-thirds of parents said that they were satisfied with their child's school and 30 percent said that they were very satisfied (Figure 6.5). There was no difference between urban school parents and rural school parents. This high level of satisfaction in part explains the low level of pressure to

Figure 6.4
Percentage of Schools, by Percentage of Students or Teachers Present on an Average Day, 2009–2010

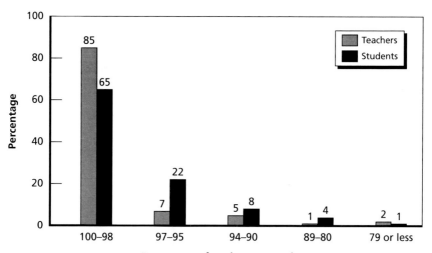

SOURCE: World Bank SBM National Survey (2010), administrative data provided by schools.
NOTE: N = 400 schools.
RAND MG1229-6.4

---

[4] The reported daily student and teacher attendance is based on administrative data provided by the principal or his or her designee.

Figure 6.5
**Percentage of Parents, by Level of Satisfaction with Their Child's School,
2010**

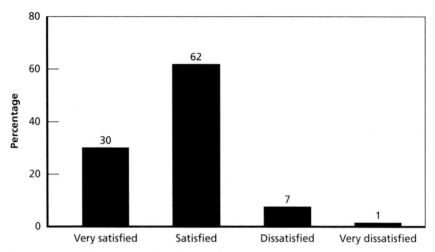

SOURCE: World Bank SBM National Survey (2010), parent survey.
NOTE: N = 2,400 parents.
RAND MG1229-6.5

improve student achievement that teachers, principals, and education
staff at all levels reported.

Low School Performance in Reading and Mathematics

During the 2009–2010 school year, fifth-grade students in all 400 sampled schools were tested in Bahasa and mathematics. The tests, developed for this study,[5] were aligned with the curriculum at this grade
level. The test was administered to about 8,100 students toward the
end of the school year.

Schools performed better in Bahasa than mathematics. About
three-quarter of schools averaged between 41 and 60 percent of correct
responses in Bahasa. The majority of schools (89 percent), on the other
hand, averaged only 21–40 percent of correct responses in mathemat-

---

[5]   Student-level achievement data were not otherwise available.

ics (Figure 6.6). The low test scores in a majority of sampled schools appear consistent with results on international tests. In the 2009 PISA, Indonesian 15-year-old students scored 49th out of 62 participating countries in reading and 53rd in mathematics (OECD, 2010).

Major Hindrances to Improving Student Achievement

In spite of the relatively low level of student achievement, few district staff, principals, or teachers consistently identified major hindrances to improving student achievement. Typically, 40 percent or less of stakeholders rated such potential hindrances as large class size, low rate of student or teacher attendance, high rate of teacher turnover, or poor teacher preparation as moderate to great (Table 6.3). Insufficient district support and capacity of district to provide professional development were similarly identified as hindrances by fewer than 40 percent

Figure 6.6
Percentage of Schools, by the Average Percentage of Items Students Correctly Responded To and by Subject, 2010

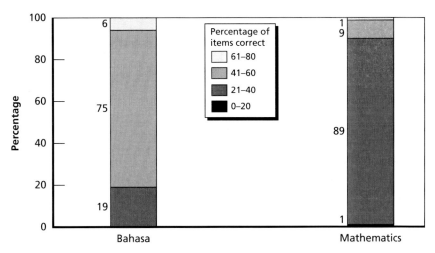

SOURCE: RAND-developed testing instrument, 2010.
NOTE: N = 400 schools and 7,916 students for Bahasa and 8,024 for mathematics.
RAND MG1229-6.6

Table 6.3
Percentage of Stakeholders Who Reported Moderate to Great Hindrances, by Type of Hindrance and Stakeholder, 2010

Hindrance to Improvement of Student Performance	District Head	Subdistrict Head	Principal	SC Chair	Teacher
Too many students in class	39	41	30	26	22
Inadequate school facilities	69	64	39	45	40
Shortage of textbooks/ instructional materials	60	59	28	38	29
Low rate of student attendance	34	28	24	24	27
Low rate of teacher attendance	40	37	22	27	DA
High rate of teacher turnover	21	21	33	21	DA
Poor teacher preparation	37	46	20	29	15
Insufficient district support	31	25	46	26	DA
Insufficient capacity of district to provide services to all schools	17	29	57	DA	DA
Insufficient capacity of district to provide professional development	20	27	37	DA	DA
Insufficient funding	74	49	DA	45	DA

SOURCE: World Bank SBM National Survey (2010), district head, subdistrict head, principal, SC chair, and teacher surveys.

NOTES: N = 54 districts, 47 subdistricts, 391 principals, 344 SC chairs, and 2,396 teachers. "DA" means "did not ask."

of stakeholders including principals, although the latter were more likely than district staff to do so.

Four potential hindrances were identified by a majority of district staff, however. Inadequate school facilities, shortage of textbooks and instructional materials, and insufficient funding were identified by about two-thirds of district and subdistrict heads. However, fewer stakeholders (28–40 percent) at the school level (principals, teachers, and SC chairs) shared this assessment, suggesting greater acceptance by principals than district staff of these conditions as unalterable, or suggesting potential complacency among school-level stakeholders.

The fourth hindrance—insufficient capacity of districts to provide services to all schools—was identified by a majority of principals. This assessment was shared by a much smaller percentage (17–20 percent) of district-level staff.

These differences in perception between district-level and school-level staff about major hindrances to improvement in student performance are similar to those identified relative to hindrances to SBM noted in Chapter Four. They suggest either a widespread acceptance of existing school conditions and student performance levels among school-level stakeholders or miscommunication of what is important at the school level and, hence, differences in priorities between the two levels of education.

Summary

Measures of intermediate outcomes in this study were limited to the perceived effects of SBM, the use of school discretionary resources, the perceived effects of the BOS program, student and teacher attendance, parental satisfaction with their child's school, and student performance.

In the case study, respondents were evenly split between those reporting that no changes had been made as a result of the implementation of SBM and those who pointed to some positive changes. The latter mainly mentioned an improved relationship with parents through an increase in the frequency of individual contacts between parents and teachers. In turn, some teachers said that they had made various changes in their instructional methods including lecturing less and engaging students in their own learning activities more, more frequent use of student groupings, and greater connection of content taught with practical experience. Also, they pointed out that more textbooks and books were now available to students. As for SC members, they mostly pointed to various types of facility improvements, ranging from repairing a leaking roof to fixing the toilets, painting the school wall, building a fence around the school, and the like.

Overall, schools spent about 60 percent of their discretionary resources on instruction-related activities, including paying for non-PNS teachers hired locally to complement the regular teacher corps, developing students' tests and reports, implementing student activities, and, to a lesser extent, providing textbooks for classrooms and the library and for staff development. However, there were wide variations across schools (although not so much across regions) in the share of total school budget spent on instruction-related activities, with some schools spending less than 20 percent and others spending more than 80 percent of their budget on such activities. About half of schools spent between 60 and 80 percent of their budget on instruction-related activities.

The effects of the BOS program were seen to be generally positive. Three-quarters of schools reported being better off financially than pre-BOS, and another 17 percent reported no change. A large majority of stakeholders of all types, including district staff, principals, teachers, and SC members, reported that BOS had a positive effect on a number of student-related and other outcomes, including higher transition rates of students to junior high school, higher enrollment of poor students, higher student performance, lower dropout rate, increased availability of textbooks, and increased school authority. At the same time, they felt that BOS had resulted in less fund-raising. This latter effect appeared to be confirmed by parents, with 90 percent reporting that they had made no monetary contributions and the remainder reporting contributions between U.S. $1 and $6 in the previous year.

Similarly, parental in-kind contributions were minimal, with one exception. Twenty percent of parents reported giving time to help maintain the school facility.

Student and teacher attendance was reportedly high. Most schools reported 98–100 percent attendance on an average day. Still, a nontrivial share of schools reported lower attendance rates, with about 8 percent of schools reporting 90 percent or lower attendance of either students or teachers on an average day.

The overwhelming majority of parents were satisfied with their child's school, in part explaining the lack of pressure to improve student achievement felt by principals, teachers, and other stakeholders, as noted above.

Students scored relatively low on the study-administered tests in Bahasa and mathematics, consistent with student achievement measured in the PISA of 2009.

Finally, we identified major differences between district and school staff in the identification of some major hindrances to school implementation of SBM and student performance improvements. These differences in perceptions suggest a potential miscommunication between districts and schools of what is important at the school level and, hence, differences in priorities between the two levels of education.

CHAPTER SEVEN
Factors Associated with SBM Implementation and Outcomes

In this chapter, we examine the relationships between school capacity and district support to implement SBM, and SBM level of implementation and outcomes. Because we expected different factors to be related to different dimensions of SBM implementation and outcomes, unique statistical models were developed to explore these relationships. We begin our discussion by describing the overall approach to our analyses and its limitations. Second, we discuss the factors associated with various measures of the level of SBM implementation. The factors found to be associated with two intermediate outcomes—the share of discretionary budget schools allocated to instruction and teacher attendance—are discussed next. Fourth, we describe the factors associated with student achievement. Finally, we provide a summary of our findings. Appendix D contains a comprehensive list and description of the factors considered in these analyses.

Methods and Limitations

We used ordinary least squares (OLS) in examining the various factors affecting implementation of school-based management practices, budget allocation, teacher attendance, and student outcomes in mathematics and Bahasa.[1] We applied district weights to the sample to

---

[1] We also used restricted maximum likelihood (REML) for analyzing factors associated with budget allocation and the results were similar.

ensure the representativeness of the elementary schools to the general population of schools; this ensured accuracy in estimating the sizes of effects and corresponding significance levels.

The analyses were conducted at the school level with the exception of a set of analyses examining student achievement in Bahasa and mathematics. Since the academic achievement analyses are at the student level, we adjusted for the fact that students are nested within schools. We accounted for variations at both the student and the school level to correct the standard errors resulting from the lack of independence of test scores of students within the same school.

Because some of the dependent measures (i.e., SBM practices) were not normally distributed, we used transformational procedures to ensure a normal distribution and minimize the effects of outliers.[2] Extreme outliers for the predictors were either excluded from the analyses or truncated by assigning them either the lowest or highest nonoutlier score. We conducted sensitivity testing by analyzing the full sample as well as the sample with excluded outliers. These analyses yielded similar results. Last, we tested for multicolinearity between different predictors by examining the variance inflation factor. None of the predictors in the final models were found to be multicolinear.

Since the OLS regression procedure assumes that all cell variances in the population are the same, we conducted a test of the homogeneity of the variance. The results show that this assumption was not fully met.[3]

A major limitation of the analyses performed in this chapter is that there was only one year of data. Our analyses therefore examined budget allocation decisions, SBM practices, and outcomes (teacher attendance and performance of students) for only school year 2009–2010. Ideally, we would need at least three years of data to be able to establish a trajectory of growth and measure the effects of cumula-

---

[2] We logged outcome measures that were negatively skewed and squared those that were positively skewed.

[3] Violation of the homogeneity assumption might lead to an underestimation of the standard errors and thus cause insignificant associations to become significant.

tive exposure to the reform. Thus, it is important that any relationship found in our modeling be interpreted as "associative" and not "causal."

Another limitation pertains to the use of survey data in our modeling of student academic achievement. Teachers and parents were not linked to their specific students or children who were tested. In our modeling, we aggregated teacher- and parent-level information (e.g., characteristics, qualifications, influence over instruction matters, involvement in school, and decisionmaking) to the school level so that we could relate this information to student achievement data. Aggregation to the school level does result in loss of variation within the variables, however, reducing their power to predict outcomes.

A third limitation has to do with the nature of surveys in general. Survey data cannot capture every aspect of a reform. In this study, the survey focused on capturing the central features of SBM; however, in the process, it might have overlooked or not measured in depth other important SBM aspects that might be associated with outcomes. For example, the surveys did not collect data on teacher behavior in the classroom as a result of SBM.[4] Similarly, the surveys did not address the effectiveness of district and other stakeholder monitoring.

Factors Associated with SBM Implementation

Central to SBM is providing schools with autonomy so that educators and school communities can make important educational decisions regarding their schools. As discussed above, schools differed in the extent to which they were autonomous and engaged in participatory decisionmaking. In this section, we examine various factors that influenced the implementation of four central SBM practices characterizing school autonomy and decisionmaking:

- *School autonomy:* measured by the number of school managerial and budgetary areas for which the principal reported that the

---

[4] However, note that we did ask about changes in instructional as well as other school practices during our case study interviews of principals and focus groups, including teachers, SC members, and parents. Our findings suggest that there were few changes in instructional and other practices (see Chapter Six).

school had made the final decision without involvement from an external stakeholder, such as the district, subdistrict, province, or central government

- *Principal influence on school managerial matters:* measured by the level of influence over managerial matters relating to the school, including developing the school vision and goals, developing the work plan, allocating discretionary total and BOS funds, hiring and firing non-PNS teachers, purchasing supplies and materials, and planning school facilities
- *Teacher influence on instruction:* measured by the level of influence over instruction, including development of syllabi, instructional materials and methods, groupings of students, and achievement tests used
- *Parental input:* measured by the number of school matters for which parents provided input.

We relied on our conceptual framework to identify the factors that may be associated with the above four measures of SBM implementation.

1. *Principal, teacher, and parent capacity.* We would expect that both principal and teacher capacity may affect the level of implementation of SBM. Principals and teachers with higher levels of education may be better prepared to make decisions on their own and be able to articulate their preferences with greater force. Those with more years of experience in managing schools or teaching, on the other hand, might be set in their ways and less malleable than new hires to adopting the new roles advocated by SBM. We would also expect that principals' self-reports of preparedness to lead the school and teachers' self-reports of preparedness to teach may affect the various measures of SBM level of implementation. Higher levels of preparedness may indicate principals' and teachers' higher level of confidence, which allows them to act independently. Additionally, parent education may be associated with increased parental voice, as parents with more education may be more able and feel more comfortable about approaching school officials and advocating for their children.

2. *Socialization and training.* We also expect that the extent to which principals and teachers received training and socialization on SBM, BOS, and other managerial and instructional matters from the districts or were otherwise supported by the district staff would be associated with SBM implementation. Further, teacher frequency of attendance in KKG and adequacy of support from the KKG may be associated with SBM implementation. KKGs provide an opportunity for teachers to learn from one another as well as to discuss and address issues that may be common across schools within a subdistrict.

3. *District influence over school matters.* We also theorize that district influence over school matters and the level of interaction with the school is associated with the extent to which schools have autonomy and the influence that principals, teachers, and parents might have over school matters.

4. *School responsiveness to parents.* The extent of transparency, i.e., openness of the school and its staff felt by parents and the information provided to parents about the school, may also be associated with parental input.

5. *School characteristics.* Finally, some school characteristics, such as school size and location, may affect the level of implementation of SBM: school size because it may be more difficult to implement SBM in larger schools (Hatry et al., 1993) and location because schools in rural areas may have less capacity and support to implement SBM.

Findings

Although similar models were run for all four measures of SBM implementation, there was little overlap in the results across them, so we discuss the factors we found associated with each of them separately (Table 7.1). At the end of this section, we highlight the few factors that were consistently, although not necessarily significantly, associated across several measures of SBM implementation.

School autonomy was negatively associated with principal education. Principals with higher education levels were more likely to involve external shareholders in final decisions regarding various school operations. As expected, higher district influence was associated with less

Table 7.1
Factors Associated with Selected Measures of SBM Implementation

Factor	School Autonomy	Principal Influence	Teacher Influence	Parental Input
District support				
Adequacy of teacher KKG	−.25		+.65***	+.32
Number of days of teacher training			+.06*	
Capacity				
Years of teaching			−.02**	
Principal education (versus high school)	−.77***	+.48**	+.11	+.07
Principal preparedness		+.89***		
Influence				
District	−.46***	+.28***		
Principal	+.44**			
School-parent relationship				
School responsiveness	−.65**	+.08	+.20	+.70**
Provision of information	−.52***		+.21*	+.41***
Region (versus Java)				
Kalimantan	−.46*	−.52***	−.54***	−.22
Papua	−.83*			
Sumatera		−.31*		
Sulawesi			−.37*	
Maluku	−.61*		−1.10***	
Urban school	−.35*	+.20	+.30	−.41*
Sample size (schools)	355	358	355	355
Explained variance (R^2)	.26	.29	.16	.17

SOURCE: Appendix E, Table E.1.

NOTES: Only statistically significant associations and nonsignificant associations that are consistent across several SBM practices are presented in this table (see Table E.1 for details). All coefficients are standardized. For instance, an increase of one standard deviation in principal education is associated with a .77 standard deviation decrease in school autonomy.

* = significant at .1, ** = significant at .05, *** = significant at .01.

school autonomy and greater principal influence was associated with more autonomy.

In addition, schools that provided more written information to parents and whose principals and teachers were more likely to listen to parent opinions were associated with less school autonomy.

Other principal and teacher capacity and socialization factors, such as teacher and principal preparedness and teacher education, were statistically nonsignificant and only weakly associated with school autonomy.

Schools in three regions—Kalimantan, Papua, and Maluku—were associated with lower school autonomy than schools in Java. This may be a result of different regional policies. Also, schools in urban areas were associated with lower levels of autonomy than schools in rural areas.

Principal influence on school management was associated with principals' higher level of education and self-reported greater preparedness to lead their schools. Principal preparedness is a measure of the confidence that principals have in their ability to lead and manage their schools and, hence, to make independent decisions for their schools. More district influence was also positively associated with more principal influence on school matters. The likely explanation for this unexpected positive association is, again, that principals continue to rely heavily on district guidance and the more they feel supported by the districts, the more influence they feel they can exercise.

No other capacity, district support (e.g., socialization), or school characteristic factors were associated with principal influence, with one exception. Schools located in Kalimantan and Sumatera, all else being equal, were less likely to have more influential principals than schools in Java and all other regions.

Teacher influence on instructional matters was positively associated with the adequacy of KKG support. The latter gives teachers opportunities to share information and experiences and provides them with instructional skills. Such skills are necessary for them to exercise control over instruction-related matters at their schools. The more training days teachers received was also, but weakly, associated with more teacher influence exerted on instructional matters.

The more years of experience teachers had was negatively, though weakly, associated with more teacher influence, suggesting that newer teachers may be more confident in exercising their influence than older teachers, who may be less comfortable with changing practices. Schools that provided parents with more information about their activities were associated with more teacher influence on instruction.

There were large regional differences in teacher influence on instructional decisions. Teachers in Kalimantan, Sulawesi, and Maluku were less likely than teachers in Java to have influence on classroom instruction.

No other factors, including teacher and principal capacity and school characteristics, were associated with teacher influence.

Parental input on various school matters was positively associated with school responsiveness to parents and information provided to parents. Also, schools in urban areas were less likely than schools located in rural areas to receive input from parents. However, this difference was barely statistically significant.

Overall, the results show that the association between school capacity and district support factors and implementation levels of each of the four SBM practices considered differed in significance, magnitude, and directionality. Few patterns across all four measures emerged from these analyses. Schools whose teachers felt that their KKG meetings were useful and that were more responsive to parents tended to be associated with more influence over managerial and instructional matters and more parental participation in school decisionmaking. Urban schools also tended to be associated with higher levels of principal and teacher influence and lower levels of school autonomy.

Factors Associated with Intermediate SBM Outcomes

As noted in Chapter Two, the expectation of SBM is that the decisions made by schools will be better aligned with student needs than decisions made under other forms of school governance. Schools' decisions should be reflected in their budgetary and programmatic decisions, principal and teacher behavior, and instructional practices—the so-called intermediate outcomes—which are expected to improve student performance. In this section, we examine the association of SBM level of implementation with two such intermediate outcomes for which we collected data: the share of discretionary budget schools allocated to instruction and teacher attendance.

Share of Discretionary Resources Allocated to Instruction

As shown in the preceding chapter, schools differed in how much of their discretionary resources they allocated to items associated with instruction, including hiring non-PNS teachers, developing and administering student tests, providing additional student programs (e.g., tutoring and after-school programs), textbooks and other books, and professional development for teachers. The share of schools' total discretionary funds allocated to instruction ranged from less than 2 percent in some schools to more than 80 percent in others (Table 6.1).

We relied on our conceptual framework (Figure 2.1) and descriptive findings to guide our specifications of factors that may be expected to relate to school budget allocation decisions.

1. *Revenue sources.* We expect that allocation of school discretionary funds to instruction may differ depending on both total funding and sources of revenues. Schools with more discretionary funds at their disposal may have more to allocate to instruction after they have committed the amount needed to cover such necessities as electricity, supplies, school maintenance (e.g., roof repairs), and furniture. Schools also received funds from different sources, including their provincial, district, and local governments, in addition to the funds they received from the central government BOS program. Although BOS funds can be spent flexibly, funds provided from other sources may impose different constraints on their use and, thus, affect the share schools have to allocate to instruction.

2. *School characteristics.* We would also expect that some school characteristics, such as school size, school location, proportion of low-income students, and parental level of education, may affect schools' resource allocation to instruction. Larger schools may achieve some economies of scale on necessities as well as on some categories of expenditures related to instruction, such as non-PNS teacher salaries and test

development. Urban schools, in turn, may be under greater pressure to increase student achievement and to prepare students for middle school. Also, schools with larger percentages of low-income students may have to spend more on student aid in the form of transportation, scholarships, or additional programs. Finally, parents with higher levels of education may be placing more direct or indirect pressure on schools to increase student achievement.

3. *Influence over school matters.* Various stakeholders may also seek to influence schools to allocate resources according to their own preferences, which may differ among teachers, districts, school committee members, and parents. Also, as noted above, different combinations of stakeholders were said to be involved in making final decisions in different schools. So, we expect different levels of influence by the various stakeholders to be associated with the allocation of resources across schools.

4. *Frequency of BOS monitoring.* The extent of transparency, i.e., the extent of monitoring and information provided to various stakeholders about school budget allocation, may also be associated with the share that is allocated to instruction.

5. *Principal capacity.* Finally, principal capacity, values, and motivations may play a role in how school resources are allocated. Although we have data on principal capacity, we did not collect information on their qualitative preferences, and thus we focus on examining principal education, experience, and certification.

Findings

Schools that received additional BOS funds from their province or district dedicated a larger share of their discretionary budget to instruction. This may be either because these schools chose to do so or because these funds came with conditions that favored expenditures for instruction (Table 7.2). By contrast, receipt of provincial aid or local revenues had the opposite association. Schools receiving such funds spent a smaller share of their discretionary budget on instruction, possibly because these funds were earmarked for specific purposes, such as facility improvements. However, the share of total funds provided by local governments and other sources was so small (less than 2 percent

Table 7.2
**Factors Associated with the Percentage of School Total
Budget Allocated to Instruction**

Factor	Share of Budget Allocated to Instruction
School characteristics	
School size	+.10**
Revenue sources (percentage of total)	
Provincial BOS	+.02***
District BOS	+.01***
Province aid	−.02***
Local revenues	−.03**
District support	
Number of teacher training days	
Adequacy of teacher training	
Capacity	
Principal education	+.05**
School-parent relationship	
School responsiveness	+.39*
Region (versus Java)	
Kalimantan	−.46***
Maluku	−.62***
Papua	−1.59***
Sample size	381
Explained variance (R^2)	.26

SOURCE: Appendix E, Table E.2.

NOTES: Only significant associations are shown on this table (for
details, see Table E.2). Coefficients are all standardized. For instance,
the .10 coefficient for school size means that an increase of one
standard deviation in school size is associated with a .10 standard
deviation increase in the share of budget allocated to instruction.

* = significant at .1, ** = significant at .05, *** = significant at .01.

of school budgets) as to not be an important factor in determining the share of funds spent on instruction.

Of the school characteristics included in the analysis, only school size was positively associated with the share schools spent on instruction, suggesting that there may be economies of scale associated with spending that is unrelated to instruction. Neither school location, parental education, nor the share of students from low-income families was associated with the share of discretionary budget spent on instruction.

The extent to which parents felt that schools were responsive to them was associated with a larger share of school expenditures spent on instruction. These schools were said by parents to provide them with opportunities to file complaints and to have a principal and teachers who were responsive to parents' opinions about school-related issues or their children's education.

A higher level of principal education was associated with a larger share of discretionary budget being spent on instruction. It may be that principals' level of education is a proxy for their values. Principals with higher education levels may see themselves as instructional leaders and not solely as administrators, and thus they may allocate a larger portion of their budget to instructional improvement. Neither teacher, school committee, and district influence nor teacher or principal capacity were associated with the share of funds schools allocated to instruction.

Schools in three regions—Kalimantan, Papua, and Maluku—were associated with allocating a smaller share of their budget to instruction than the average schools in Java and other regions, suggesting regional differences in policies or practices.

Overall, only about one-third of the variation in school budget allocation to instruction was accounted for by the factors for which data were available. One possibly important missing independent variable in this analysis was school needs. We would expect that variations in school needs (e.g., whether schools need improvement in facilities or instructional programs) would be a significant driver of schools' budget allocation decisions. We would also expect that previous years' allocation decisions would affect any one year's budget allocation, suggesting that future analysis of these decisions ought to be viewed over time rather than over just one year as we were constrained to do.

Teacher Attendance

Teacher attendance was measured by the share of teachers present on an average day as reported by the school. As in previous analyses, we relied on our conceptual model to identify relevant factors that might affect teacher attendance.

1. *Principal and teacher capacity.* We expect more qualified principals to promote a school culture that is conducive to teacher morale, thus increasing teacher attendance. Similarly, we expect qualified teachers to be better equipped to cope with the challenges of teaching and thus more committed to showing up regularly to school.

2. *Socialization and training.* Principals who received more leadership training may be expected to promote a more favorable school climate and, hence, higher teacher attendance. Similarly, teachers who are provided with more training and feedback regarding their instruction may feel more supported and, thus, more committed to their school.

3. *Influence over school management and instruction.* Districts and principals exerting higher levels of influence on school decisions, especially on instruction, may lead to more teacher dissatisfaction and, hence, lower teacher attendance.

4. *School autonomy.* Teachers in schools with lower levels of autonomy are likely to have less influence in their classroom, possibly affecting their attendance.

Findings

Only two of the factors included in this analysis were found to be associated with teacher attendance: number of teacher district training days and adequacy of district training (Table 7.3). However, contrary to our expectations, the association was negative, suggesting that these variables were proxies for some other factors affecting teacher attendance not included in the model, such as accessibility to the school.

Teacher attendance differed by region. Teachers in Kalimantan and in Maluku were less likely to be present than in schools in Java and other regions.

Table 7.3
Factors Associated with Teacher Attendance

Factor	Teacher Attendance
District support	
Number of teacher training days	−.06**
Adequacy of teacher training	−.18*
Region (versus Java)	
Kalimantan	−.28**
Maluku	−.86**
Papua	
Sample size	354
Explained variance (R^2)	.16

SOURCE: Appendix E, Table E.3.

NOTES: Only significant associations are shown on this table (for details see Table E.3). Coefficients are all standardized.

* = significant at .1, ** = significant at .05.

That few factors were associated with teacher attendance may also be in part due to measurement errors. The data on teacher attendance were collected from school administrators and may not be accurate.

Factors Associated with School Achievement

Student achievement in Bahasa and in mathematics was measured by a test that we developed and administered to fifth-grade students. In addition to factors found in past research to be associated with student achievement, we also included in this analysis factors suggested by our conceptual framework to be associated with student achievement.

1. *Family characteristics.* Findings from previous studies of student achievement lead us to expect that gender, family income, and parental education would affect student achievement (Coleman et al., 1966; Zellman et al., 2009).

2. *Principal and teacher capacity.* We would also expect principal and teacher capacity, such as education, certification, length of experience, and preparedness, to be positively associated with student achievement (Darling-Hammond, 2000; Goldhaber and Brewer, 2000; Monk, 1989). Better-prepared principals and teachers should be more likely to foster more effective student instruction, leading to better student outcomes.

3. *Influence over school management and instruction.* We also expect principal and teacher level of influence to be associated with student achievement. Teachers who have influence over their classroom instruction may be better able to address their students' academic needs and, consequently, to improve academic achievement.

4. *School autonomy.* The theory of SBM is that schools are better equipped than remote stakeholders to identify students' academic needs. Hence, the more that schools have control over decisions, especially pertaining to instruction, the more they may be expected to be associated with higher student achievement.

5. *Instructional expenditures.* We would also expect that higher expenditures spent on instruction (e.g., tutoring) would be associated with higher student achievement.

6. *Standards and hours of instruction.* Higher academic standards and longer hours of instruction would also be expected to be associated with higher levels of student achievement.

Findings

Many of the variables expected to be associated with school average student achievement actually were. Boys were more likely to score lower than girls, but in Bahasa only. As expected, higher parental education was associated with higher student achievement in both Bahasa and mathematics (Table 7.4).

Similarly, the more that principals were prepared to lead their school, the greater the number of certified teachers in the school; also, years of experience were associated with higher student achievement in both Bahasa and mathematics.

Schools that used curriculum standard level 4 (equivalent to international standards) were also more likely than other schools to be

Table 7.4
Factors Associated with Student Achievement

Factor	Bahasa	Mathematics
Student and family characteristics		
Student gender (versus girls)	−.30***	
Parent education	+.17***	+.07*
Student attendance	+.02***	+.03**
Capacity		
Teacher certification	+.06**	+.07***
Years in teaching	+.03***	+.01**
Principal preparedness	+.13*	+.76**
Curriculum standard level 4 (versus standard level 1)		+.28*
Region (versus Java)		
Kalimantan		−.17*
Papua		−.23*
Bali	−.37***	
Sulawesi	−.18*	−.23**
Maluku	−.40**	
Sample size (students/teachers)	7,164 / 348	7,350 / 355
Explained variance (R^2)	.18	.07

SOURCE: Appendix E, Table E.4.

NOTES: Only statistically significant associations are shown in this table (for details see Table E.4). Coefficients are all standardized. For instance, the −.30 coefficient on student gender means that an increase in the number of boys relative to the number of girls by one standard deviation is associated with a .30 standard deviation decrease in the school score in Bahasa.

* = significant at .1, ** = significant at .05, *** = significant at .01.

associated with higher student achievement in mathematics. However, this is likely due to self-selection of higher-performing students in these schools.

There were several regional differences in student achievement. Students in Sulawesi were less likely than students in Java to perform well in both Bahasa and mathematics. Schools in Bali and Maluku were less likely to perform well only in Bahasa, and schools in Kalimantan and Papua were less likely to perform well in mathematics, all relative to students in Java.

Of equal interest were the factors found not to be associated with student achievement. These include teacher feedback from district supervisors, the amount of funds spent per student on instruction, school autonomy, and the influence exercised by principals, teachers, and districts. One potential reason for this lack of association with these variables related to SBM implementation is that there has been little change in behavior and instructional practices as a result of SBM, as reported in previous chapters.

Summary

Few of the many school capacity and district support factors examined were found to be associated with our measures of SBM implementation, the share of school budget allocated to instruction, teacher attendance, or student achievement. Schools that provided information on school activities to parents were associated with a larger share of their discretionary funds spent on instruction, with less autonomy, and with receiving more input from parents.

Higher principal education was associated with higher principal influence on school operations and a larger share of discretionary budget spent on instruction, and principals who were better prepared to lead were associated with higher principal influence on school operations and higher student achievement. In this study, principal preparedness is a self-reported measure of how well principals are prepared to provide leadership, plan for school academic improvements, make decisions on school curriculum, and supervise and evaluate teachers.

In turn, the average number of training days teachers received at a school and the usefulness of KKG meetings were associated with higher teacher influence and more parental input. At the same time, certified teachers were also associated with higher student achievement.

Last, it should be noted that none of the SBM measures of implementation and the schools' share of discretionary budget spent by schools on instruction were associated with student achievement. It may be that implementation of SBM so far has not resulted in significant enough changes in school practices, as suggested in the other chapters of this report.

CHAPTER EIGHT

Conclusions and Recommendations

This study describes the nationwide status of SBM implementation in Indonesia and explores its effects on selected school intermediate and student performance outcomes. In this chapter, we outline our main conclusions and our recommendations for improving both. In reaching our conclusions, we had to weigh responses to questions that were inconsistent across different respondents. In these cases, we considered the likelihood that the various respondents might have provided socially desirable answers. We generally gave more weight to respondents who were less likely to do so. For instance, when considering quantity of principal and teacher training, we gave more weight to the amount reported by school staff than to the amount districts reported they provided. Similarly, when considering conflicting responses between case study and survey respondents, we gave more weight to the former, because we were able to ask for follow-up clarification from case study respondents.

Also, we recognize that our data are for only one point in time (2009–2010), and we do not know whether the practices we describe represent changes from practices in previous years. Nevertheless, the descriptions and analyses presented in this report provide a more comprehensive insight than ever before into how SBM is currently practiced in Indonesia and the implementation challenges encountered.

Conclusions

Overall, decentralization of school decisions to the school level has been achieved, at least from the perspective of school staff. However, the participation of school committees and more generally of parents in school decisions and school affairs remains to be achieved. Similarly, achieving full transparency remains a work in progress. Although school staff perceived that they had autonomy to make independent decisions, we found little evidence that they took advantage of it by making independent significant instructional and operational changes in their schools. Part of the problem may be principals' and teachers' lack of knowledge and confidence about taking risks to make independent decisions. Districts continued to exercise a great deal of influence on school decisions, and principals and teachers continued to defer to them for the most part. Also, both principals and teachers felt that they received inadequate support and training on SBM and on how to make school performance improvements. Finally, we found no evidence that SBM implementation to date was associated with student performance, in part because of weak overall implementation or lack of change in instruction. To address this question more definitely will require collecting data over several years.

School autonomy over operational, budgetary, and programmatic decisions has been achieved, at least in the eyes of principals and teachers. Most principals reported that they had the authority to make final decisions on key school operations, including the setting of the school's vision, developing medium-term and annual plans, formulating budgets, and performing school maintenance. They also reported having autonomy over instructional issues, including the curriculum, textbooks, and student promotion. The majority of teachers agreed and, in addition, said that they had full autonomy in their classroom over their choice of instructional methods, groupings of students, and sequence in which they taught the curriculum. More than two-thirds of principals said that they could also make independent decisions in the recruitment and hiring of teachers, even though these functions continue to be the responsibility of the central government, at least for PNS teachers. It may be that principals were mainly referring to their choosing and hiring of non-PNS teachers, who accounted for one-third of the teacher force in 2010.

Setting the school calendar was the only school operational decision that nearly one-half of principals said was not in their purview to make, remaining the responsibility of the district.

Although schools had autonomy on all key school operations, they were reluctant to use it. Most principals and teachers indicated that they had not taken advantage of the autonomy they have to make significant programmatic or instructional changes. When they sought to make changes, they generally consulted and asked for approval from either their district supervisor or appropriate staff. Principals said that they rarely made decisions on their own and that they welcomed, and often needed, district guidance in all aspects of their school operations. This reluctance of schools to go it alone seems to be confirmed by the high level of influence districts continued to exercise in many areas of school managerial and programmatic decisions, as reported by both principals and district staff. Another indicator of the reluctance of schools to make independent decisions was the uniformity of their stated goals and priorities and the similarity of actions they were taking to improve performance. Indeed, most schools reported that they had not made significant changes as a result of SBM.

We did not explore the reasons for this reluctance to act independently. Some principals hinted that they were afraid to make mistakes or to appear arrogant and authoritarian. A potential institutional reason was the strong tendency for clusters of schools (usually at the subdistrict level) to adopt uniform policies and practices. However, possibly two more important reasons may be a strong sense of respect for authority and school stakeholders' insufficient knowledge and expertise to make policy and program changes, as a majority of principals and district staff indicated.

Principals typically consulted with other educators before making a decision; however, school committees and parents were rarely actively involved. In the majority of schools, principals nearly always consulted with teachers, and often with district staff and principals of other schools in their cluster, before making a decision. However, SC members were rarely actively involved in their school's decisionmaking process, including in the setting of their school's mission, the preparation of the school's plans, and the allocation of BOS funds. The common practice was for the SC chair to be asked to review and sign off on the decision after the school had made it final—which the chair nearly always did without asking questions. The attitude of principals was to consider the SC as just an intermediary to inform parents of school decisions and, in turn, the attitude of SC members was one of no interference and deference to school staff. Lack of knowledge about school affairs and lack of availability of SC members during the day were other reasons given for the lack of involvement of SCs in school affairs.

Parents were similarly rarely involved in their children's school affairs, for both institutional and personal reasons. Most schools did not hold meetings with parents to discuss school matters other than to invite them to pick up their children's report cards, nor did they formally provide them with information on school decisions and activities. In turn, school committee members reported rarely holding any meetings with parents to seek their input, in part, they said, because few parents could attend during the day. As for parents, their attitude was, "At school, children are the teachers' responsibility—at home the parents'."

Transparency of information and accountability external to school were minimal. The lack of involvement in school affairs by SC members and parents and minimal sharing of information by schools suggest that transparency of school decisions was minimal. And, as noted above, SC members rarely actively questioned decisions made by the school, even when its chair was required to sign off on them.

Monitoring of school activities, although said to take place with some frequency by districts and principals, was seemingly rarely used for effective accountability or for providing support for improvements. District staff said that schools were monitored about monthly; however, according to principals and teachers, these visits were not as frequent and focused heavily on administrative matters. District supervisors did observe teacher instruction and student discipline in the classroom; however, a majority of teachers reported never receiving feedback or receiving it only once or twice a year. Additionally, when supervisors gave feedback, it was more in terms of what teachers should do (e.g., increase student achievement, increase their creativity, increase their use of visual aids, or improve their students' attendance) and less on how they should do it. In addition, most principals and teachers reported feeling no or little pressure from parents to increase student performance.

Nevertheless, school staff placed a high priority on attempting to have all sixth-grade students pass the National Exam, and they typically provided out-of-school time to prepare these students for it. They also felt a competitive pressure for their school to perform well. This self-imposed "accountability" could be strengthened as a major accountability tool by setting progressively higher targets for the desired percentage of students graduating and by providing incentives and sanctions for meeting the target.

The capacity to implement SBM differed across schools but overall was low. The capacity to implement change in any organization depends on the amount of discretionary resources available and understanding of the programmatic requirements for the change. We found that discretionary funding available to schools (net of PNS teacher salaries and benefits) differed broadly, with some schools reporting less funding than they were supposed to get under the central government BOS program (about U.S. $43 per student) and some schools receiving far in excess of it. The latter schools received additional BOS funds and aid from their district or provincial governments.

Principals, teachers, and SC members said that they had insufficient understanding of the concept of SBM and of the functions attributed to SCs, possibly contributing to the mixed implementation of SBM by schools. For instance, they understood SBM's theory and overall purposes (school autonomy, community participation) but not necessarily the responsibilities and the required actions they implied. Also, most principals and SC members had some misconceptions regarding the expected functions of the SC. In addition, a majority of principals said that they were not adequately prepared to provide effective leadership and a vision for school staff, plan for school academic improvements, and develop a curriculum, and, hence, they were not prepared to develop alternatives to their existing practices. Similarly, a majority of teachers reported that they were not adequately prepared to plan effective lessons or to use varied instructional methods. District staff members, including supervisors, were even less positive about principal and teacher preparation.

Few principals and teachers received sufficient assistance or training during the school year; however, many said they needed it. A majority of principals and teachers said that they had not received training. When they had, it was insufficient in key areas associated with SBM, including developing a school's vision and plans, making best use of budget resources, and developing a curriculum. Similarly, about two-thirds of teachers said that they had received no training or that the training they received was insufficient in such areas as instructional methods, subject matter, and planning lessons.

Socialization of SC members about their roles and responsibilities was even more sporadic, with half of districts not offering such training and most SC members reporting not receiving any socialization over the past two years.

When asked to identify the three most important things that would make their school better, principals and teachers most frequently mentioned improvements to the school's physical facility and support for teachers. The school upgrades desired ranged from more chairs and tables or classrooms for students to rooms for a library, laboratory, or health unit. The support desired for and by teachers included more training on teaching methods, academic content, and thematic approaches to teaching the curriculum. It also included having greater access to such teaching props as maps, scales, visual aids, and science and mathematics kits.

How well principals are prepared to lead and how well teachers are trained were associated with better SBM-related outcomes and higher student achievement. Higher principal education was associated with higher principal influence on school operations and a larger share of discretionary budget being spent on instruction, and principals better prepared to lead were positively associated with higher principal influence on school matters and higher student achievement. Principal preparedness is a self-report of how well principals were prepared to provide effective leadership, plan for school academic improvements, make decisions on school curriculum, and supervise and evaluate teachers. In turn, the greater the number days of training teachers received and the more the KKG meetings were useful to them, the higher the teacher influence. Also, teachers who were credentialed were associated with higher student achievement as measured in this study.

Schools that offered opportunities for parents to file complaints and were responsive to parents' opinions and feedback and schools that provided information on school activities to parents were associated with a larger share of a school's discretionary budget being spent on instruction and more input being received from parents. Also, schools receiving resources from their provincial and district governments in addition to those received from the central government BOS program were more likely to allocate a greater share of their total resources to instruction. However, not all schools received such additional resources, leading to wide differences across schools in the amount they had available per student.

Last, none of our SBM-implementation-related measures and the share of budget schools spent on instruction were associated with student achievement. It may be that implementation of SBM has not yet resulted in significant changes in school operational and instructional practices, as suggested in other chapters of this report.

Recommendations

Improving the implementation and outcomes of SBM in Indonesia will require overcoming insufficient school stakeholders' knowledge of SBM and SC responsibilities and developing their capacity to make independent operational and instructional changes. It will also require changes in the attitudes of all stakeholders about their respective roles in school affairs. To address these issues, consideration should be given to the following three areas:

- expanding SC, principal, and teacher capacity to implement SBM
- increasing schools' ability to make managerial and instructional changes
- developing district capacity to support schools and SBM.

For each of these areas, we offer a set of specific measures that policymakers may consider individually or in combination.

Expanding SC, Principal, and Teacher Capacity to Implement SBM

Expand SC Ability to Participate in School Affairs. We recommend considering four options to expand the SC's ability to participate in school decisions.

Make it easier for SC members to participate. SC members as well as school staff said that they rarely met, because SC members were not available during school hours. A simple solution to this issue is to require that school staff meet with the SC during hours convenient for their members. At the same time, SC members could be provided with an incentive to participate in the form of a small stipend to cover their transportation and other meeting costs.

Upgrade the knowledge of SC members. SC members reported receiving no or little training regarding their functions and how to fulfill them and not having access to detailed guidelines regarding their roles and responsibilities. To effectively participate in school affairs, SC members should receive training about the goals and purposes of SBM, the multiple SC functions as defined by central government guidelines, and how to fulfill these functions. They also need to be given basic training on how to conduct meetings, develop a school vision, and engage in participatory planning and budgeting. SC members should be provided with specific guidelines on the kind of school indicators they should monitor to assess school activities. The above knowledge and guidelines should be codified in a manual made available to SC members for easy reference. Elements of the above training were developed and tested by the DBE1 demonstration program, providing a potential model for providing this training (USAID, 2010). To be effective, training will need to be ongoing and of sufficient intensity.

Increase the authority of the school committee. To accomplish this, several measures to provide the SC with increasingly greater authority over school affairs may be considered, including:

- Clarify the policy regarding SC fund-raising activities: Most SCs and schools behave as if fund-raising from parents were prohibited, taking away an important role that SCs played in the past and a way of more actively involving parents in supporting their schools. If it was not the intent of the central government to entirely do away with local school and SC fund-raising, as we believe, this should be communicated clearly.

- Link the school and SC with the village council: Pradhan et al. (2011) have shown the potential that reaching out to education stakeholders outside the school committee—and especially in seeking the village council's cooperation in supporting school improvements and including village council representation on the SC—has in improving student learning, although not necessarily SC involvement.

- Give the SC authority over allocation of BOS funds and the hiring and firing of principals and teachers: Programs that have given school committees this authority have been found to increase council and parental participation in school matters, including school planning and administration of the budget (Jimenez and Sawada, 2003; Arcia, Porta Pallais, and Laguna, 2004). Providing such high-stakes authority to SCs, however, would require ensuring that SC members have the qualifications and knowledge to make the necessary judgments.

Provide the SC, parents, and the public with comparative information on the performance of schools. Beyond the report card, which provides only information on the performance of an individual child, parents and the community do not receive additional information on their school's performance or activities, including classroom size, academic and extracurricular programs, and other school activities. In particular, they do not receive information on their school's performance and offerings compared to those of other schools in their locality, district, and the nation. Performance information can readily be derived from the national assessment standardized tests administered by the Ministry of National Education, and other school information could be collected centrally as well. In the context of Indonesia, which offers school choice, this information would help parents to make a more informed decision on their choice of school and could promote more competition across schools.[1] It could also provide SCs and parents with a greater incentive to hold their school accountable and motivate them and the public more generally to demand and support school improvements (Bruns, Filmer, and Patrinos, 2011; Stecher et al., 2010; Vernez et al., 2009).

Upgrade Principal and Teacher Capacity to Implement SBM. To increase the capacity of principals and teachers to implement SBM, we recommend considering the following four measures.

Provide principal leadership training. With SBM, the principal is the most important stakeholder. Principal leadership quality is second only to teacher quality in contributing to student learning (Leithwood, Anderson, and Wahlstrom, 2004; Waters, Marzano, and McNulty, 2003). His or her example and actions determine the extent to which school decisions will be broadly participatory and focused on managerial and instructional improvements (Knapp, Copland, and Talbert, 2003). The objective of principal leadership training should be to provide an understanding and full appreciation of the practices that make effective leaders.

Provide principals and teachers with professional development on SBM, the SC role, and effective SBM practices. Principals and teachers alike reported not understanding what SBM required of them, and many did not fully grasp the participatory and oversight role of the SC or the role of the teaching board. In addition to being provided professional development in these areas, both principals and teachers need to develop skills in conducting activities that are key in supporting SBM, including how to conduct school and student needs assessments; formulate a school's vision, mission, and objectives; engage in participatory planning; develop a curriculum; prepare a budget; and implement school improvements. This latter component—how to prepare and manage the implementation of change—is often neglected in professional development. To be most effective, this professional

---

[1] Of course, school performance is only one among many factors that parents consider in choosing a school for their children, including convenience of location and their child's preference, which often trump the relative performance and other characteristics of the school (Vernez et al., 2009).

development should be provided to all teachers in a school or cluster of schools at the same time. Teachers who participate in training collectively are more likely to reinforce what was learned and implement changes (Borko, 2004; Desimone et al., 2002; Garet et al., 2001; USAID, 2010).

Clarify the authority devolved to the school. As noted in Chapter One, the SBM guidelines decreed by the Ministry of National Education are ambiguous, leaving room for the district to continue to play its traditional directive role over schools. As we found, schools are generally shy to do anything that may not be approved by their district. The standards for SBM should be clarified to unambiguously indicate devolvement of authority to schools. The role of the district should be limited to that of enabler and monitor of SBM implementation and school performance (see the section "Develop District Capacity to Support SBM," below).

Broaden school autonomy. Principals have de jure, if not de facto, autonomy over most key managerial and instructional matters, except the ability to hire and fire teachers. PNS teachers continue in large measure to be hired and assigned by the central government. Given that the quality of teachers plays a significant role in setting the conditions for student learning and that teachers represent 80 to 90 percent of school "resources," this lack of principals' authority over teachers represents a major limitation to the practice of SBM. Consideration should be given to devolving this authority to the school. This would not be new to principals. They already have been hiring and overseeing non-PNS teachers who are used to complement PNS teachers assigned to them by the central government. In addition to gaining more authority over a critical school resource, principals would gain more flexibility to balance their teacher workforce with their programmatic needs.

Increase Schools' Ability to Make Managerial and Instructional Changes

The measures discussed above may lead to increased participation of stakeholders in school planning and decisions but not necessarily in programmatic, curriculum, or instructional changes, which would be expected to more directly affect student learning. This is because principals and teachers may not know how to improve student learning and may be unprepared to try alternative approaches to their routine practices. In our assessment of the status of SBM, we found that many principals and teachers did not have the necessary knowledge and basis for taking local initiatives. To increase schools' ability to implement curriculum and instructional changes, we recommend considering the following three measures.

Assess the Need for and Provide Professional Development. When teachers were asked in the case study what was the most important support they needed to make their school better, most answered that they needed more training in academic content, teaching methods, and thematic approaches to teaching the curriculum. The research literature suggests that a teacher's knowledge of his or her subject matter has been associated with higher student achievement (Hill, Rowan, and Ball, 2005; Yoon et al., 2007; Glewwe and Kremer, 2005; Clewell et al., 2004). With regard to instruction, teachers could potentially choose among different approaches. Currently, Indonesian teachers are also being asked to use a student-centered form of teaching, so-called active learning or PAKEM (Robert, 2009; USAID, 2011). However, few teachers have received training on how to apply it in the classroom or to their particular subject (USAID, 2010). Research in schools in various countries that encouraged student-centered learning[2] found that when teachers tried to use this practice without fully understanding what it entailed, they could feel overwhelmed and the result could be poorer instruction (Zellman et al., 2009; Contreras and Talavera Simoni, 2003).[3] The research literature also suggests that the most effective teaching methods are those that deliver instruction in a clear and structured way, including providing an overview of course content at the beginning of the class, organizing course content in a step-by-step sequence, stressing key points, pausing briefly at appropriate times

---

[2] Student-centered learning refers to a model of teaching that is generally represented by minimal teacher lecturing, small group activities that engage students in problem solving, and frequent questions and discussion.

[3] To date, studies have produced limited evidence that student-centered instruction results in better learning outcomes (Richardson, 2003; Din and Whitley, 2007; Le et al., 2009; Wilson et al., 2010).

to assess student comprehension, and reviewing course content periodically during and at the end of class (Scheerens, 2004; Chilcoat, 1989; UNESCO, 2006).

Given limited resources, determining what needs to be emphasized in professional development related to subject content and teaching methods would be important. Hence, we recommend that a teacher professional development needs assessment be conducted first, to help set priorities. To maximize the benefits of professional development, research suggests that all teachers in a single school or cluster of schools should be trained at the same time, instead of the current approach of providing training to one or two teachers and expecting that the knowledge acquired may be transferred. As noted above, teachers who participate in training collectively are more likely to reinforce what was learned and implement new instructional approaches in the classroom.

Expand Access to Teaching Aids. Other support that teachers said they needed to improve the quality of their schools includes having greater access to teaching props, ranging from simple maps, scales, and visual aids to science and mathematics kits. These props help students understand concepts visually and may lead to gains in instructional time as teachers are able to move more quickly from one topic to the next.

Address Resource Disparities Among Schools. Effective development and implementation of programmatic improvements (e.g., increased instructional hours, after-hours tutoring, smaller classroom size, and staff development) depend in part on whether schools have the necessary resources to finance them. As this study found, schools differ markedly in the discretionary resources available to them, in part because of the uneven contributions made by provinces and districts. This raises the question of the role that each level of government (provincial, district, and local) ought to play in financing education. A first step in addressing this question would be to collect more detailed information regarding the current financing of education by districts and provinces and their fiscal capacity.

Develop District Capacity to Support SBM

Providing the support necessary to upgrade school stakeholders' capacity to implement SBM, as suggested above, will require altering the role of the district to that of an enabler of change. In this role, districts will need to expand their capacity to provide ongoing technical assistance and staff development to principals, teachers, and SC members as outlined above. As noted by our respondents, providing socialization for one or two days over a one-year period, as is the current practice, is usually not sufficient for stakeholders to fully understand the changes required in their actions. And as the DBE1 demonstration program showed, training needs to be provided to all key stakeholders in the schools at the same time instead of to one or two participants per school at a time and expecting, unrealistically, that the knowledge gained by a few stakeholders will be transferred to all other stakeholders (USAID, 2010). In this new role, district supervisors' functions should principally become to monitor school SBM implementation and improvements and provide technical assistance and mentoring. Ensuring that principals and teachers have ongoing access to expert advice and consultation after training is completed has been shown to be more effective than training alone (Klein, 2004; Plevyak, 2007; Joyce and Showers, 2002). To take on this role, supervisors themselves will need to be provided with adequate training before they can provide this ongoing support.

Incremental Implementation of Recommendations

Emphasis placed on developing SC and school capacity and altering the role played by districts will require both time and additional resources. Also, we are cognizant that although our recommendations are based on research best practices, they have not always been consistently found to be effective in all cultural and educational environments. With limited resources and the uncertain effectiveness of the recommended actions in the context of Indonesian schools, we recommend that policymakers carefully set priorities on which recommendations to implement and in which sequence and implement the selected measures experimentally and incrementally involving a limited number of districts and schools at a time to learn about the implementation challenges and issues involved and ascertain effectiveness. For instance, we recommend that the restructuring of the role of the district be implemented in a few districts and schools in clusters within those districts. Once experience has been gained in a few districts, potential implementation issues addressed, and effectiveness ascertained, implementation could be expanded to a few more districts and schools at a time. We recommend using a similar approach with individual or groups of recommendations made to improve SC and parent participation in school affairs.

Sampled Districts

Table A.1
Sampled Districts

No.	Region	No.	District or Municipality	District	Total No. of Public Elementary Schools in District	Total No. of Public Elementary Schools in Region	Min. No. of Elementary Schools per District	Max. No. of Elementary Schools per District
3	Bali/NTB	1	D	Kupang	211	7,467	60	691
		2	D	Manggarai Barat	90			
		1	M	Denpasar	179			
4	Papua	1	D	Yahukimo	44	933	2	105
		2	D	Sorong	91			
		1	M	Sorong	43			
6	Sulawesi	1	D	Minahasa Selatan	177	13,608	20	670
		2	D	Bantaeng	133			
		3	D	Enrekang	211			
		4	D	Luwu	209			
		5	D	Polewali	333			
		1	M	Gorontalo	108			
7	Sumatera	1	D	Padang Pariaman	426	28,571	10	813
		2	D	Indragiri Hulu	231			
		3	D	Rokan Hulu	267			

Table A.1—Continued

No.	Region	No.	District or Municipality	District	Total No. of Public Elementary Schools in District	Total No. of Public Elementary Schools in Region	Min. No. of Elementary Schools per District	Max. No. of Elementary Schools per District
		4	D	Batangharil	190			
		5	D	Tanjung Jabung Barat	188			
		6	D	Musi Banyuasin	137			
		7	D	Lampung Barat	264			
		8	D	Rejang Lebong	167			
		9	D	Kaur	100			
		10	D	Karimun	131			
		1	M	Payakumbuh	99			
		2	M	Tanjung Balai	56			
5	Maluku	1	D	Kepulauan Aru	64	1,776	29	306
		2	D	Halmerhera Utara	71			
		1	M	Tidore Kepulauan	156			
1	Java	1	D	Bogor	1,458	63,349	11	2,486
		2	D	Sumedang	557			
		3	D	Garut	1,382			

Table A.1—Continued

No.	Region	No.	District or Municipality	District	Total No. of Public Elementary Schools in District	Total No. of Public Elementary Schools in Region	Min. No. of Elementary Schools per District	Max. No. of Elementary Schools per District
		4	D	Purwakarta	434			
		5	D	Purbalingga	464			
		6	D	Kebumen	835			
		7	D	Boyolali	595			
		8	D	Semarang	513			
		9	D	Brebes	883			
		10	D	Sleman	389			
		11	D	Gresik	457			
		12	D	Tuban	617			
		13	D	Ngawi	615			
		14	D	Kediri	610			
		15	D	Tulungagung	621			
		16	D	Pasuruan	700			
		17	D	Lumajang	574			
		18	D	Pamekasan	546			

Table A.1—Continued

No.	Region	No.	District or Municipality	District	Total No. of Public Elementary Schools in District	Total No. of Public Elementary Schools in Region	Min. No. of Elementary Schools per District	Max. No. of Elementary Schools per District
		19	D	Sumenep	612			
		20	D	Serang	978			
		1	M	Jakarta Barat	455			
		2	M	Tegal	126			
		3	M	Blitar	52			
2	Kalimantan	1	D	Pulang Pisau	148	10,435	27	489
		2	D	Tanah Laut	227			
		3	D	Pasir	227			
		1	M	Singkawang	72			

SOURCE: 2008 Census of Schools, Indonesian Ministry of Higher Education.

Memo on Specifications for Grade 5 Student Tests in Bahasa and Mathematics

September 9, 2009

To: Hahja Umar, Director, Institut Asesmen Indonesia

From: Georges Vernez, RAND Corporation

Subject: Specifications for Grade 5 Student Achievement Test Development

Overall Description of Requested Work

The consultant will develop standardized tests in (1) mathematics and (2) Bahasa Indonesia for grade 5 (primary) students. The length of the tests should not exceed 45 minutes.

The tests will be used as part of a larger study on school based management that will be conducted during the 2009–10 school year. The purpose of the testing is to provide an indicator of school performance based on student test scores, not to measure curriculum implementation in Indonesia. The students will be drawn from a nationally representative sample that will include both urban and rural as well as very poor districts and communities.

The tests must be completed by November 1, 2009, subject to approval.

Test Specifications

- Both standardized tests should be based on the official curriculum for grade five in each subject.
- Because the actual application will take place between March and May 2010, so content areas that are covered at the end of the school year should not be included (if relevant).
- Both tests should use multiple choice or simple fill-in answer items to facilitate marking and data entry; no open ended writing or computational activities should be used.
- Both test (mathematics and Bahasa) should have an introduction page where 2–3 example items are provided students. In addition, a script to help test enumerators explain to students the correct process for completing the test booklet should be provided.
- The tests should be included in a single test booklet. No cover page needs to be included. The first page of the booklet should include practice examples for the Bahasa test (with script as noted see above), followed by the Bahasa test itself. After the last question on the language test a warning for students to stop work should be inserted, and there should also be a separating page between the language and mathematics tests so that enumerators can verify that students have stopped working on the language test and are not moving ahead with mathematics. The mathematics test should follow and begin with a new set of 2–3 practice items for students to complete based on instructions from the enumerator (using the script).
- Test length should be about 45 minutes maximum per subject, not including the practice items and explanation/instructions provided by the enumerators. There is no required minimum or maximum number of questions. The whole process including instructions and example items should take a maximum of two (2) hours.
- Two forms for each test should be developed to help insure test security during the application. The two forms can be nearly identical in terms of content areas, item difficulty, and sequencing, and should have the same practice items and instructions. There

is no need for matrix sampling of item areas by form in order to cover more areas of the curriculum. The two forms should have a sufficient number of anchor items to permit equating of scores post-test (ideally at least 6 anchor items).

- There are no specific requirements for item difficulty or goals for proficiency levels. In general, items which are likely to be either very easy or very difficult for the average grade 5 student should be avoided. However, the main criterion for item inclusion is that the content is part of the official curriculum, and is likely to have been taught in grade 5 between July and March of the school year or in previous grades.
- An item key with correct answers should be provided for marking the test booklet after the final application.

Characteristics of PNS and Non-PNS Teachers

PNS teachers are civil servants hired, paid, and assigned to schools by the Ministry of National Education. Non-PNS teachers are hired locally directly by schools using BOS program funds. Overall, about one-third of all teachers are non-PNS.

Although PNS teachers are somewhat more educated than non-PNS teachers, they appear to be substitutes for one another. PNS and non-PNS teachers reported spending the same number of hours in the classroom and the same number of hours at school. They taught the same subjects, although non-PNS teachers were somewhat more likely than PNS teachers to teach English (Table C.1).

However, PNS teachers were more likely to teach in grades 5 and 6, whereas non-PNS teachers were more likely to teach in grades 2 and 3. PNS teachers were more likely than non-PNS teachers to counsel students and provide out-of-hours lessons to students, but the differences are not large.

A question often asked in Indonesia is whether there are too many teachers overall. Although our data cannot answer this question conclusively, two comparisons are suggestive of an affirmative answer.

The Indonesian student-teacher ratio averaged 16 and class size averaged 26 for a 1.6 ratio of class size to student per teacher. In California schools, where the average class size is in the same range as in Indonesia, this ratio is lower, ranging between 1.2 and 1.4.

The reported average number of hours spent in the classroom (16) relative to the number of hours spent at school (28) also suggests that Indonesian teachers may not spend enough time in the classroom. In the United States, teachers spend most of their school time in the classroom teaching.

Table C.1
Selected Characteristics of PNS and non-PNS Teachers

Characteristic	PNS	Non-PNS
Education		
First/second diploma—teaching education	57%	79%
Bachelor of teaching	42%	20%
Hours per week teaching	30	28
Hours per week at school	17	16
Subject taught		
Bahasa	96%	95%
Mathematics	96%	95%
English	6%	17%
Duties other than teaching		
Student counseling	82%	64%
Monitor students	31%	4%
Additional lessons for students	80%	65%
Administration	83%	64%
Grade taught		
Grade 1	50%	50%
Grade 2	33%	67%
Grade 3	38%	62%
Grade 4	47%	53%
Grade 5	59%	41%
Grade 6	67%	33%

SOURCE: World Bank SBM National Survey (2010).
NOTE: N = 2,352 teachers.

Definitions of Variables

Table D.1
Percentage and Average Scores for School Characteristics, Practices, and Outcomes

Variable	Description	Sample Size	Percentage or Average	Standard Error
Dependent variables				
SBM implementation				
School autonomy	Number of operational areas for which decisions were made without external involvement	400	7.50	0.12
Principal influence on operations	Principals' influence score over 11 operational areas (scale ranges from 1 to 4; 1 = no influence and 4 = very influential)	400	3.25	0.03
Teacher influence on instruction	Teachers' influence score over 9 instructional areas (scale ranges from 1 to 4; 1 = no influence and 4 = very influential)	396	3.10	0.02
Parental voice	Number of operational areas for which parents provided input	400	2.60	0.14

Table D.1—Continued

Variable	Description	Sample Size	Percentage or Average	Standard Error
Share of discretionary budget spent on instruction	Percentage of discretionary budget spent on instruction	400	59.60%	0.31
Teacher attendance	Percentage of teachers present daily as reported by school in 2010–2011	390	97.40%	0.39
Student achievement				
Bahasa	Percentage of correct Bahasa test responses	7,916	47.08%	0.17
Mathematics	Percentage of correct math test responses	8,024	30.99%	0.14
Independent variables				
School characteristics				
Student enrollment	Size of school's student population	400	181.67	5.80
Curriculum standards	Percentage of schools with:	400		
	Regular standards (Standard 1)		78.00%	
	Pilot schools with national standards (Standard 2)		7.00%	
	National standards (Standard 3)		14.00%	
	Pilot schools with international standards (Standard 4)		1.00%	
Hours per week for subject				
	Hours of Bahasa instruction per week	388	5.55	
	Hours of math instruction per week	397	5.56	0.06
Urban schools	Percentage of schools located in urban areas	400	19.00%	0.06

Table D.1—Continued

Variable	Description	Sample Size	Percentage or Average	Standard Error
Share of revenue sources	Percentage of total discretionary budget from:			
Provincial BOS	Provincial BOS	400	1.60%	
District BOS	District BOS	400	3.40%	
Province aid	Province aid	400	3.10%	
District aid	District aid	400	5.20%	
Local revenues	Local revenues	400	1.00%	
Other	Other sources	400	3.30%	
Per-student expenditures	Amount of per-student expenditures (U.S. dollars)	400	72.61	
Student/family characteristics				
Student gender	Percentage of male students	8,046	50.00%	
Students from low-income families	Percentage of students from low-income families	400	49.96%	1.58
Parent education	Parent educational level (scale ranges from 1 to 11; 1 = "did not complete primary school" and 11 = "postgraduate")	398	2.96	0.06
Parent pressure	Extent to which parents put pressure on schools (scale ranges from 0 to 4; 0 = no pressure and 4 = intense pressure)	400	1.59	0.07
Attendance				
Teacher attendance	Percentage of teachers present daily as reported by schools	390	97.36%	0.39
Student attendance	Percentage of students present daily as reported by schools	375	97.04%	0.18

Table D.1—Continued

Variable	Description	Sample Size	Percentage or Average	Standard Error
District support				
Teacher received feedback from district	Teachers receiving feedback from district (scale ranges from 1 to 6; 1 = never and 6 = always)	392	2.94	0.04
Principal training	Number of training days received by principal	389	3.40	0.18
Adequacy of principal training	Extent to which principal training was sufficient (scale ranges from 0 to 3; 0 = did not receive training and 3 = sufficient training)	400	0.97	0.05
Frequency principal met with district	Number of times principal met with district in the current year	386	9.70	0.33
Teacher training	Number of training days received by teachers	398	2.09	0.10
Adequacy of KKG training	Extent to which teacher KKG training was sufficient (scale ranges from 1 to 4; 1 = no training and 4 = sufficient training)	386	3.49	0.02
Capacity				
Teacher certification	Percentage of schools with certified teachers	400	45.50%	
Teacher experience	Years of teacher experience in any school	400	17.12	0.34
Teacher preparedness	Extent to which teachers self-reported that they were well prepared in various activities related to instruction (scale ranges from 1 to 4; 1 = not prepared and 4 = very well prepared)	399	3.48	0.01
Teacher education	Teacher educational level (scale ranges from 1 to 11; 1 = "did not complete primary school" and 11 = "postgraduate")	400	6.05	0.06

Table D.1—Continued

Variable	Description	Sample Size	Percentage or Average	Standard Error
Teacher received feedback	Teachers receiving feedback from principal either orally or in writing (0 = no and 1 = yes)	400	0.77	0.01
Principal education	Percentage of principals with following educational level:	400		
	1 = high school diploma		9.00%	
	2 = some college (levels I–III)		37.00%	
	3 = college degree and above		54.00%	
Principal experience	Years of principal experience in any school	400	8.05	0.38
Principal preparedness	Extent to which principal self-reported being prepared to lead (scale ranges from 1 to 4; 1 = not prepared and 4 = very well prepared)	400	3.41	0.02
Principal certification	Percentage of principals certified	400	50.00%	
Principal knowledge of BOS	Number of BOS goals identified correctly by principals out of a maximum of 7 options	400	4.80	0.06
School committee knowledge of SC	Number of SC goals identified by SC committee out of a maximum of 6 options	400	2.47	0.06
Hindrances to SBM	Extent to which various school factors hinder implementation of SBM (scale ranges from 1 to 4; 1 = no hindrance and 4 = lots of hindrance)	400	2.09	0.04
Influences				
School autonomy	Number of operational areas for which decisions were made without external involvement	400	7.50	0.12
Teacher influence on instruction	Teachers' influence score over 9 instructional areas (scale ranges from 1 to 4; 1 = no influence and 4 = very influential)	396	3.10	0.02

Table D.1—Continued

Variable	Description	Sample Size	Percentage or Average	Standard Error
Principal influence	Principals' influence score over 11 operational areas (scale ranges from 1 to 4; 1 = no influence and 4 = very influential)	400	3.25	0.03
Parent input	Number of school operations (out of 10) for which parents provided input	400	2.60	0.14
District influence	District influence score over 11 operational areas (scale ranges from 1 to 4; 1 = no influence and 4 = very influential)	400	2.81	0.04
School committee influence in management	SC influences score over 11 operational management areas (scale ranges from 1 to 4; 1 = no/little influence and 4 = lots of influence)	393	2.16	0.04
Other				
External entities involved in BOS decisions	Percentage of districts or subdistricts involved in school decisionmaking regarding BOS	399	31.00%	
School has BOS team	Percentage of schools with a BOS team	399	71.00%	
Frequency of BOS monitoring				
By school committee	Frequency of BOS monitoring (scale ranges from 1 to 6; 1 = never and 6 = weekly)	396	3.09	0.06
By district	Frequency of BOS monitoring (scale ranges from 1 to 6; 1 = never and 6 = weekly)	396	3.28	0.06
School-Parent Relationship				
School responsiveness to parents	Extent to which parents agreed that schools were responsive to them (scale ranges from 1 to 4; 1 = strongly disagree and 4 = strongly agree)	400	3.33	0.01

Table D.1—Continued

Variable	Description	Sample Size	Percentage or Average	Standard Error
Information provided to parents	Percentage of schools providing information to parents on students or school activities	400	59.00%	
Region	Percentage of schools in:	400		
Java	Java		43.00%	
Sumatera	Sumatera		22.00%	
Bali	Bali		5.00%	
Kalimantan	Kalimantan		8.00%	
Sulawesi	Sulawesi		11.00%	
Maluku	Maluku		6.00%	
Papua	Papua		5.00%	

Factors Associated with Intermediate SBM and Student Outcomes

Table E.1
Factors Associated with SBM Implementation

Factor	School Autonomy	Principal Influence	Teacher Influence	Parental Voice
School characteristics				
Student enrollment	−0.01	<0.01	<0.01	<0.01
Parent education	−0.01	0.03	0.08	−0.03
Urban school	−0.35*	0.20	0.30	−0.41*
District support				
Principal training	0.01	0.01	−0.01	−0.02
Adequacy of principal training	0.09	−0.03	−0.09	0.03
Frequency principal met with district	−0.02	<0.01	0.01	0.02
Teacher training	−0.03	−0.01	0.06*	0.04
Adequacy of KKG training	−0.25	−0.24	0.65***	0.32
Capacity				
Principal education (versus high school)	0.77***	0.48**	0.11	0.07
Principal education (some college)	−0.45	0.37	0.28	0.25

Table E.1—Continued

Factor	School Autonomy	Principal Influence	Teacher Influence	Parental Voice
Principal experience	0.01	<0.01	<0.01	<0.01
Principal preparedness	0.11	0.89***	−0.05	0.06
Principal knowledge of BOS	0.09	0.04	0.04	−0.02
Teacher education	−0.09	−0.01	−0.03	0.02
Teacher experience	0.02	<0.01	−0.02**	−0.01
Teacher preparedness	−0.60	0.16	0.35	−0.23
Hindrances to SBM	−0.08	0.04	−0.02	−0.06
Influence				
Principal	0.44**			0.15
Teacher	0.03			0.19
District	−0.46***	0.28**	−0.04	0.03
School-parent relationship				
School responsiveness to parents	−0.65**	0.08	0.20	0.70**
Information provided to parents	−0.52***	−0.06	0.21*	0.41***
Region (versus Java)				
Sumatera	−0.32	−0.31*	−0.20	−0.23
Bali	−0.38	−0.33	−0.20	0.20
Kalimantan	−0.46**	−0.52***	−0.54***	−0.22
Sulawesi	−0.06	−0.13	−0.37*	0.31
Maluku	−0.61**	−0.35	−1.13***	−0.50
Papua	−0.83*	0.41	0.33	0.07
Sample size (schools)	355	358	355	355
Explained variance (R^2)	0.26	0.29	0.16	0.17

SOURCE: World Bank SBM National Survey (2010).

NOTE: All coefficients are standardized relative to standard deviation, i.e., expressed in terms of effect size.

* = significant at .1, ** = significant at .05, *** = significant at .01.

Table E.2
Factors Associated with the Percentage of Discretionary Budget
Allocated to Instruction

Factor	Standardized Regression Coefficient
School characteristics	
Student enrollment	+.10**
Percentage of students from low-income families	−.03
Parent education	−.04
Urban school	+.32
Share of discretionary budget (percentage of total)	
Provincial BOS	+.02***
District BOS	+.01***
Province aid	−.02***
District aid	<.01
Local revenues	−.03**
Other	−.02***
Capacity	
Principal education	+.05**
Principal experience	<.01
Principal preparedness	−.10
Principal certification	−.04
School committee knowledge of SC	−.01
Influence	
Teacher	−.15
District	+.08
School Committee	−.08
School-parent relationship	
School responsiveness to parents	+.39*

Table E.2—Continued

Factor	Standardized Regression Coefficient
Frequency of BOS monitoring	
By school committee	−.06
By district office	+.02
Other	
External entities involved in BOS decisions	−.13
School had BOS team	−.02
Region controls	
Sumatera	+.05
Bali	−.05
Kalimantan	−.46***
Sulawesi	−.08
Maluku	−.62***
Papua	−1.59***
Sample size (schools)	381
Explained variance (R^2)	26

SOURCE: World Bank SBM National Survey (2010).

NOTE: All coefficients are standardized relative to standard deviation, i.e., expressed in terms of effect size.

* = significant at .1, ** = significant at .05, *** = significant at .01.

Table E.3
Factors Associated with Teacher Attendance

Factor	Teacher Attendance
School characteristics	
Student enrollment	<0.01
Parent education	0.01
Urban school	0.02
District support	
Principal training	<0.01
Adequacy of principal training	−0.02
Teacher training	−0.06**
Adequacy of KKG training	−0.18*
Feedback received by teacher	<0.01
Capacity	
Principal education (versus high school)	−0.19
Principal education (some college)	−0.05
Years as principal	<−0.01
Principal preparedness	−0.06
Teacher education	−0.10
Years of teaching	<0.01
Teacher preparedness	0.05
Teacher feedback received from principal	0.23
Influence	0.05
Principal	0.02
Teacher	0.10
District	0.03
Region (versus Java)	
Sumatera	−0.18
Bali	−0.20

Table E.3—Continued

Factor	Teacher Attendance
Kalimantan	−0.28**
Sulawesi	−0.35
Maluku	−0.86**
Papua	−1.43
Sample size (schools)	354
Explained variance (R^2)	0.16

SOURCE: World Bank SBM National Survey (2010).

NOTE: All coefficients are standardized relative to standard deviation, i.e., expressed in terms of effect size.

* = significant at .1, ** = significant at .05.

Table E.4
Factors Associated with Student Achievement

Factor	Bahasa	Mathematics
School characteristics		
Student enrollment	<0.01	<0.01**
Standard 2	0.06	−0.14
Standard 3	0.06	0.13
Standard 4	0.05	0.28*
Per-student expenditures	<0.01	<0.01
Hours per week for subject	−0.05	0.04
Urban school	0.05	0.05
Student/family characteristics		
Student gender	−0.29***	0.02
Percentage of students from low-income family	<0.01***	<0.01*
Parent education	0.17***	0.08***
Parent pressure	<0.01	−0.02
Attendance		
Student	0.03***	0.03***
Teacher	−0.01	<0.01***
District support		
Teacher received feedback from district	0.03	0.01
Capacity		
Teacher certification	0.06**	0.07***
Years of teaching	0.03***	0.01***
Teacher preparedness	−0.16	−0.19
Principal education level 2	0.10	0.17
Principal education level 3	0.12	0.12
Principal preparedness	0.13*	0.17**
Teacher received feedback from principal	0.04	<0.01

Table E.4—Continued

Factor	Bahasa	Mathematics
Influence		
Teacher	0.02	0.05
Principal	0.05	0.01
School autonomy	−0.06	−0.02
Region (versus Java)		
Sumatera	0.06	−0.12
Bali	−0.37***	0.02
Kalimantan	0.13	−0.17*
Sulawesi	−0.18*	−0.23**
Maluku	−0.40**	−0.11
Papua	−0.30	−0.23*
Sample size (students / schools)	7,164 / 348	7,350 / 355
Explained variance (R^2)	0.18	0.07

SOURCE: World Bank SBM National Survey (2010).

NOTE: All coefficients are standardized relative to standard deviation, i.e., expressed in terms of effect size.

* = significant at .1, ** = significant at .05, *** = significant at .01.

Bibliography

Allen, L., and C. Glickman (1992). "School Improvement: The Elusive Faces of Shared Governance." *NASSP Bulletin, 76,* 542, 80–87.

Arcia, G., E. Porta Pallais, and J. R. Laguna (2004). *"Otro Vistazo a la Autonomia Escolar de Nicaragua: Aceptación y Percepción en 2004."* Study for the Ministry of Education, Culture, and Sports, Managua, Nicaragua.

Bandur, A. (2007). *A Review of Development in School-Based Management in Indonesia.* Institute of Indonesia Tenggara Studies, Working Paper 3.

Barrera-Osorio, F., T. Fasih, and H. A. Patrinos, with L. Santibanez (2009). *Decentralized Decision-Making in Schools: The Theory and Evidence on School-Based Management.* Washington, D.C.: World Bank.

Benveniste, L., and J. Marshall (2004). "School Grants and Student Performance: Evidence from the EQIP Project in Cambodia." Unpublished manuscript. Washington, D.C.: World Bank.

Berends, M. (2000). "Teacher-Reported Effects of New American Schools Designs: Exploring the Relationships to Teacher Background and School Context." *Educational Evaluation and Policy Analysis, 22,* 1, 65–82.

Berends, M., S. J. Bodilly, and S. N. Kirby (2002). *Facing the Challenges of Whole-School Reform: New American Schools After a Decade.* Santa Monica, Calif.: RAND Corporation, MR-1498-EDU. As of December 18, 2011: http://www.rand.org/pubs/monograph_reports/MR1498.html

Bifulco, R. (2002). "Addressing Self-Selection Bias in Quasi-Experimental Evaluations of Whole-School Reform: A Comparison of Methods." *Evaluation Review, 26,* 5, 545–572.

Bjork, C. (2003). "Local Responses to Decentralization Policy in Indonesia." *Comparative Education Review, 47,* 2, 1–27.

Borko, H. (2004). "Professional Development and Teacher Learning: Mapping the Terrain." *Educational Researcher, 33,* 8, 3–15.

Bruns, B., D. Filmer, and H. A. Patrinos (2011). *Making Schools Work: New Evidence on Accountability Reforms.* Washington, D.C.: World Bank.

Caldwell, B. (2005). *School-Based Management.* Paris: The International Institute for Educational Planning; Brussels: The International Academy of Education, UNESCO, Education Policy Series 3.

Caldwell, S. D., and F. H. Wood (1988). "School-Based Improvement—Are We Ready?" *Educational Leadership, 42,* 2, 50–83.

Chaudhury, N., and D. Parajuli (2010). "Giving It Back: Evaluating the Impact of Devolution of School Management to Communities in Nepal." Unpublished manuscript. Washington, D.C.: World Bank.

Chilcoat, G. W. (1989). "Instructional Behaviors for Clearer Presentations in the Classroom." *Instructional Science, 18,* 289–314.

Clewell, B. C., C. Cosentino de Cohen, P. B. Campbell, and L. Perlman (2004). *Review of Evaluation Studies of Mathematics and Science Curricula and Professional Education Models.* GE Foundation.

Coleman, S. J., E. Q. Campbell, C. J. Hobson, F. MacPartland, A. M. Mood, and F. D. Weinfeld (1966). *Equality of Educational Opportunity.* Washington D.C.: U.S. Government Printing Office.

Contreras, M. E., and M. L. Talavera Simoni (2003). *The Bolivian Education Reform 1992–2002: Case Studies in Large-Scale Education Reform.* Country Studies, Education Reform and Management Publication Series, 2, 1. Washington, D.C.: Education Section, Human Development Department, World Bank.

Cuban, L. (1998). "How Schools Change Reforms: Redefining Reform Success and Failure." *Teacher College Record, 99,* 3, 453–477.

Darling-Hammond, L. (2000). "Teacher Quality and Student Achievement: A Review of State Policy Evidence." *Education Policy Analysis Archives, 8, 1 Entire Issue.* As of December 18, 2011: http://epaa.asu.edu/epaa/v8n1/2000

Datnow, A. (2005). "The Sustainability of Comprehensive School Reform Models in Changing District and State Contexts." *Educational Administration Quarterly, 41,* 1, 121–153.

Datnow, A., and J. Castellano (2000). "Teachers' Responses to Success for All: How Beliefs, Experiences, and Adaptations Shape Implementation." *American Educational Research Journal, 37,* 3, 775–799.

Datnow, A., G. Borman, and S. Springfield (2000). "School Reform Through a Highly Specified Curriculum: Implementation and Effects of the Core Knowledge Sequence." *Elementary School Journal, 101,* 2, 167–191.

David, J. L. (1989). "Synthesis of Research on School-Based Management." *Educational Leadership, 46,* 8, 45–53.

Desimone, L. M., et al. (2002). "Effects of Professional Development on Teachers' Instruction: Results from a Three-Year Longitudinal Study." *Educational Evaluation and Policy Analysis, 24,* 2, 81–112.

Din, F. S., and F. W. Whitley (2007). "A Literature Review of the Student-Centered Teaching Approach: National Implications." *National Forum of Teacher Education Journal, 17,* 1–17.

Duflo, E., P. Dupas, and M. Kremer (2007). "Peer Effects, Pupil-Teacher Ratios, and Teacher Incentives: Evidence from a Randomization Evaluation in Kenya." Unpublished manuscript. Abdul Latif Jameel Poverty Action Lab (JPAL), Cambridge, Mass.: Massachusetts Institute of Technology.

Duflo, E., P. Dupas, and M. Kremer (2009). "Additional Resources versus Organizational Changes in Education: Experimental Evidence from Kenya." Unpublished manuscript. Abdul Latif Jameel Poverty Action Lab (JPAL), Cambridge, Mass.: Massachusetts Institute of Technology.

Firman, H., and B. Tola (2008). "The Future of Schools in Indonesia." *Journal of International Cooperation in Education, 2,* 1, 71–84.

Fullan, M. (2001). *The New Meaning of Educational Change,* 3rd edition. New York: Teachers College Press.

Fullan, M. (2008). *The Six Secrets of Change.* San Francisco, Calif.: Jossey-Bass.

Garet, J. S., et al. (2001). "What Makes Professional Development Effective? Results from a National Sample of Teachers." *American Educational Research Journal, 38,* 4, 915–945.

Gertler, P., H. A. Patrinos, and M. Rubio-Codina (2006). "Empowering Parents to Improve Education: Evidence from Rural Mexico." Policy Research Working Paper 3935. Washington, D.C.: World Bank.

Glennan, T. K. (1998). *New American Schools After Six Years.* Santa Monica, Calif.: RAND Corporation, MR-945-NAS. As of December 18, 2011: http://www.rand.org/pubs/monograph_reports/MR945.html

Glennan, T. K., S. J. Bodilly, J. Galegher, and K. A. Kerr (2004). *Expanding the Reach of Education Reforms: Perspectives from Leaders in the Scale-Up of Educational Interventions.* Santa Monica, Calif.: RAND Corporation, MG-248-FF. As of December 18, 2011: http://www.rand.org/pubs/monographs/MG248.html

Glewwe, P., and M. Kremer (2005). *Schools, Teachers, and Education Outcomes in Developing Countries.* CID Working Paper 122. Cambridge, Mass.: Center for International Development, Harvard University.

Goldhaber, D., and D. Brewer (2000). "Does Teacher Certification Matter? High School Teacher Certification Status and Student Achievement." *Education Evaluation and Policy Analyses, 22,* 2, 129–145.

Grauwe, A. D. (2004). "School-Based Management (SBM): Does It Improve Quality?" Paper commissioned for the EFA Global Monitoring Report 2005, The Quality Imperative. United Nations Educational, Scientific and Cultural Organization.

Hatry, H. P., E. Morley, B. Ashford, and T. N. Wyatt (1993). *Implementing School-Based Management: Insights into Decentralization from Science and Math Departments.* Washington, D.C.: The Urban Institute.

Heyward, M., R. A. Cannon, and Sarjono (2011a). *Implementing School-Based Management in Indonesia.* Research Triangle Park, N.C.: RTI Press.

Heyward, M., R. A. Cannon, and Sarjono (2011b). "Implementing School-Based Management in Indonesia: Impact and Lessons Learned." *Journal of Development Effectiveness, 3,* 3, 371–388.

Hill, H. C., B. Rowan, and D. L. Ball (2005). "Effects of Teachers' Mathematical Knowledge for Teaching Achievement." *American Educational Research Journal, 42,* 2, 371–406.

Jimenez, E., and Y. Sawada (2003). "Does Community Management Help Keep Kids in Schools? Evidence Using Panel Data from El Salvador's EDUCO Program." Discussion paper, Center for International Research on the Japanese Economy, University of Tokyo.

Joyce, B., and B. Showers (2002). *Student Achievement Through Staff Development.* Alexandria, Va.: Association for Supervision and Curriculum Development.

Khattri, N., C. Ling, and S. Jha (2010). "The Effects of School-Based Management in the Philippines: An Initial Assessment Using Administrative Data." Policy Research Working Paper 5248. Washington, D.C.: World Bank.

Klein, M. (2004). "The Premise and Promise of Inquiry Based Mathematics in Pre-Service Teacher Education: A Poststructuralist Analysis." *Asia Pacific Journal of Teacher Education, 32,* 1, 35–47.

Knapp, M. S., M. A. Copland, and J. E. Talbert (2003). *Teaching for Learning: Reflective Tools for School and District Leaders.* Seattle, Wash.: Center for the Study of Teaching and Policy, University of Washington, February.

Le, V.-N., et al. (2009). "A Longitudinal Investigation of the Relationship Between Teachers' Self-Reports of Reform-Oriented Instruction and Mathematics and Science Achievement." *Educational Evaluation and Policy Analysis, 31,* 200–220.

Leithwood, K., and T. Menzies (1998). "Focus and Effects of School-Based Management: A Review." *Educational Policy, 12,* 325, 325–346.

Leithwood, K., K. S. Louis, S. Anderson, and K. Wahlstrom (2004). *How Leadership Influences Student Learning.* Minneapolis, Minn.: Center for Applied Research and Educational Improvement, University of Minnesota.

Levine, D. U. (1991). "Creating Effective Schools: Findings and Implications from Research Practice." *Phi Delta Kappan, 72,* 5, 389–393.

Lindle, J. C. (1996). "Lessons from Kentucky About School-Based Decision Making." *Educational Leadership, 53,* 4, 20–23.

McLaughlin, M. W., and D. C. Philips (1991). *Evaluation and Education: A Quarter Century.* Chicago: University of Chicago Press.

Ministry of National Education (2007). *Standards for Education Management by Primary and Secondary Education Units.* Jakarta, Indonesia.

Ministry of National Education (2010). *Technical Manual on BOS Funds for the Fiscal Year 2011.* Jakarta, Indonesia.

Monk, D. H. (1989). "The Education Production Functions: Its Evolving Role in Policy Analysis." *Educational Policy and Evaluation Analysis, 11,* 1, 31–45.

Murnane, R. J., J. B. Willet, and S. Cardenas (2006). "Did the Participation of Schools in Programa Escuelas de Calidad (PEC) Influence Student Outcomes?" Working paper. Cambridge, Mass.: Harvard University Graduate School of Education.

Nationmaster (2011). *Southeast Asia—Indonesia—Education.* As of December 1, 2011:
http://www.nationmaster.com/country/id-indonesia/edu-education

Organisation for Economic Co-operation and Development (OECD) (2010). *PISA 2009 Results: What Makes a School Successful? Resources, Policies, and Practices (Volume IV).* As of November 9, 2011:
http://www.oecd-ilibrary.org/education/pisa-2009-results-what-makes-a-school-successful_9789264091559-en

Osalov, L. B. (1994). "Site-Based Decision Making Councils in Kentucky Schools: Theory vs. Reality." *The Delta Kappa Gamma Bulletin, 61,* 24–30.

Oswald, L. J. (1995). "School-Based Management." Eugene, Or.: Oregon School Study Council and ERIC Clearinghouse on Educational Management.

Paes de Barros, R., and R. Mendonca (1998). "The Impact of Three Institutional Innovations in Brazilian Education." In *Organization Matters: Agency Problems in Health and Education in Latin America,* ed. W. D. Savedoff. Washington, D.C.: Inter-American Development Bank.

Parker, C. E. (2005). "Teacher Incentives and Student Achievement in Nicaraguan Autonomous Schools." In *Incentives to Improve Teaching,* ed. E. Vegas. Washington, D.C.: World Bank.

Peterson, D. (1991). *School-Based Management and Student Performance.* ERIC Digest No. 62. University of Oregon, Clearinghouse on Educational Management.

Plevyak, L. H. (2007). "What Do Pre-Service Teachers Learn in an Inquiry-Based Science Methods Course?" *Journal of Elementary Science Education, 19,* 1, 1–13.

Pradhan, M., D. Suryadarma, A. Beatty, M. Wong, A. Alishjabana, A. Gaduh, and R. P. Artha (2011). *Educational Quality Through Enhancing Community Participation: Results from a Randomized Field Experiment in Indonesia.* Jakarta, Indonesia: World Bank, East Asia and Pacific Region. WPS-5795.

Ravitch, D., and J. Viteritti (1997). *New Schools for a New Century.* New Haven, Conn.: Yale University Press.

Richardson, V. (2003). "Constructivist Pedagogy." *Teachers College Record, 105,* 9, 1623–1640.

Robert (2009). "Student-Centered Active Learning in Basic Education." *Education in Indonesia,* June 2009. As of November 8, 2011:
http://robert-aceh.blogspot.com/2009/07/student-centred-active-learning-in.html

Rodriguez, T. A., and J. R. Slate (1995). *Site-Based Management: A Review of the Literature, Part II: Past and Present Status.* As of December 1, 2011:
http://www.usca.edu/essays/vol152005/Slate2.pdf

Rogosa, D. R. (1995). "Myths and Methods: Myths about Longitudinal Research plus Supplemental Questions." In *The Analysis of Change,* ed. J. M. Gottman. Mahwah, N.J.: Lawrence Erlbaum.

Rowan, B., E. Camburn, and C. Barnes (2004). "Benefiting from Comprehensive School Reform: A Review of Research on CSR Implementation." In *Putting Pieces Together: Lessons from Comprehensive School Reform Research,* ed. C. Cross. Washington, D.C.: National Clearinghouse for Comprehensive School Research.

Scheerens, J. (2004). *Review of School and Instructional Effectiveness Research.* Paris: United Nations Educational, Scientific and Cultural Organization.

Skoufias, E., and J. Shapiro (2006). "The Pitfalls of Evaluating a School Grants Program Using Non-Experimental Data." Policy Research Working Paper 4036. Washington, D.C.: World Bank.

SMERU Research Institute (2006). *A Rapid Appraisal of the PPKS-BBM Education Sector: School Operational Assistance* (BOS). Jakarta, Indonesia.

SMERU Research Institute (2008). *Qualitative Baseline Study for PNPM Generasi and PKH.* Jakarta, Indonesia.

Stecher, B., F. A. Camm, C. Damberg, L. S. Hamilton, K. J. Mullen, C. D. Nelson, P. Sorensen, M. Wachs, A. Yoh, G. Zellman, and K. Leuschner (2010). *Toward a Culture of Consequences: Performance-Based Accountability Systems for Public Services.* Santa Monica, Calif.: RAND Corporation, MG-1019. As of December 18, 2011:
http://www.rand.org/pubs/monographs/MG1019.html

Stine, D. U. (1992). *How to Build a Leadership Team for Effective Decision Making: Tips for Principals.* Reston, Va.: Virginia National Association of Secondary School Principals.

Stringfield, S., M. A. Millsap, and R. Herman (1997). *Urban and Suburban/Rural Special Strategies for Educating Disadvantaged Children: Findings and Policy Implications of a Longitudinal Study.* Baltimore, Md.: Johns Hopkins University.

Sumintono, B. (2009). "School-Based Management Policies and Practices in Indonesia: A Study of the Implementation of the Educational Decentralization Policy at State Secondary Schools in Matoram, Lombok, Indonesia." Köln, Germany: LAP LAMBERT Academic Publishing.

Sweeting, E., M. Furaidah, and S. Koes (2007). *Three Studies: Role of School Principal; Role of School Committee; Change in Proboliuggo District, Managing Basic Education Project.* As of August 1, 2011:
http://mbeproject.net/report.html

Swirk Interactive Schooling (2010). *Indonesia: Understanding Our Nearest Neighbors.* As of December 1, 2011:
http://www.skwirk.com.au/p-c_s-1_u-149_t-453_c-1610/education/nsw/usie/indonesia-understanding-our-nearest-neighbours/culture

UNESCO (2006). *Teachers and Educational Quality: Monitoring Global Needs for 2015.* Montreal, Canada.

USAID (2010). *Implementing School-Based Management in Indonesia: The DBE1 Experience: 2005–2010.* Jakarta, Indonesia.

USAID (2011). *Decentralized Basic Education 2.* As of November 8, 2011:
http://indonesia.usaid.gov/en/USAID/Activity/185/Decentralized_Basic_Education_2

Vernez, G., R. Karam, L. T. Mariano, and C. DeMartini (2006). *Evaluating Comprehensive School Reform Models at Scale: Focus on Implementation.* Santa Monica, Calif.: RAND Corporation, MG-546-EDU. As of December 18, 2011:
http://www.rand.org/pubs/monographs/MG546.html

Vernez, G., S. Naftel, K. Ross, K. C. LeFloch, C. Beighly, and B. Gill (2009). *State and Local Implementation of the No Child Left Behind Act: Volume VII—Title I School Choice and Supplemental Educational Services: Final Report.* Washington, D.C.: Department of Education.

Walker, E. M. (2002). "The Politics of School-Based Management: Understanding the Process of Devolving Authority in Urban School Districts." *Education Policy Analysis Archives, 10,* 33. As of May 17, 2012:
http://epaa.asu.edu/epaa

Waters, T., R. J. Marzano, and B. McNulty (2003). *Balanced Leadership: What 30 Years of Research Tells Us About the Effect of Leadership on Student Achievement.* Aurora, Colo.: Mid-Continent Research for Education and Leadership.

Wilson, C. D., et al. (2010). "The Relative Effects and Equity of Inquiry-Based and Commonplace Science Teaching on Students' Knowledge, Reasoning, and Argumentation." *Journal of Research in Science Teaching, 47,* 276–301.

Wohlstetter, P., and A. Odden (1992). "Rethinking School-Based Management Policy and Research." *Education Administration Quarterly, 128,* 529–549.

World Bank (2004). *Education in Indonesia: Managing the Transition to Decentralization.* Report No. 29506. Washington, D.C.

World Bank (2007). *What Is School-Based Management?* Washington, D.C.

World Bank (2011a). *World Bank and Education in Indonesia.* As of December 1, 2011:
http://go.worldbank.org/KDPLTBFSI0

World Bank (2011b). *Independent Monitoring Report: BOS Program Implementation 2008–2009.* Jakarta, Indonesia: World Bank Office.

Yoon, K. S., T. Duncan, S. W. Lee, B. Scarloss, and K. L. Shapley (2007). *Reviewing the Evidence on How Teacher Professional Development Affects Student Achievement.* Washington, D.C.: U.S. Department of Education Institute of Education Sciences.

Zellman, G., G. W. Ryan, R. Karam, L. Constant, H. Salem, G. C. Gonzales, N. Orr, C. A. Goldman, H. Al-Thani, and K. Al-Obeidli (2009). *Implementation of the K–12 Education Reform in Qatar's Schools.* Santa Monica, Calif.: RAND Corporation, MG-880-QATAR. As of December 18, 2011:
http://www.rand.org/pubs/monographs/MG880.html